THE FURRY MENAGERIE
A COLORING BOOK

BY
ASHLEY HOLOHAN

Printed in the United States of America
ISBN 978-1633186965

TO NIUS, BLACKIE, AZURA, AND PEZ,
AND ALL THE FOLKS FROM MY STREAMS.

YOU ALL INSPIRE ME!

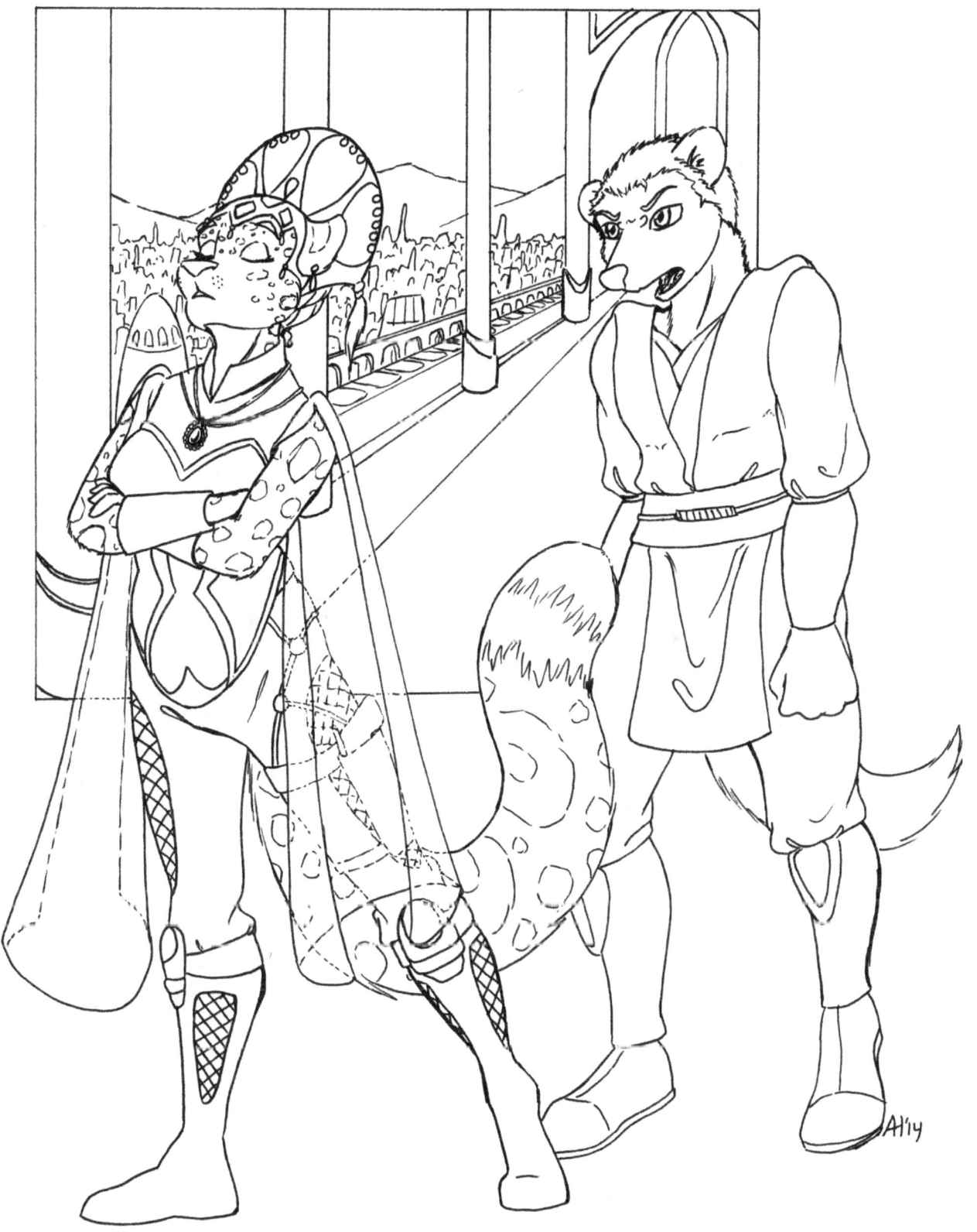

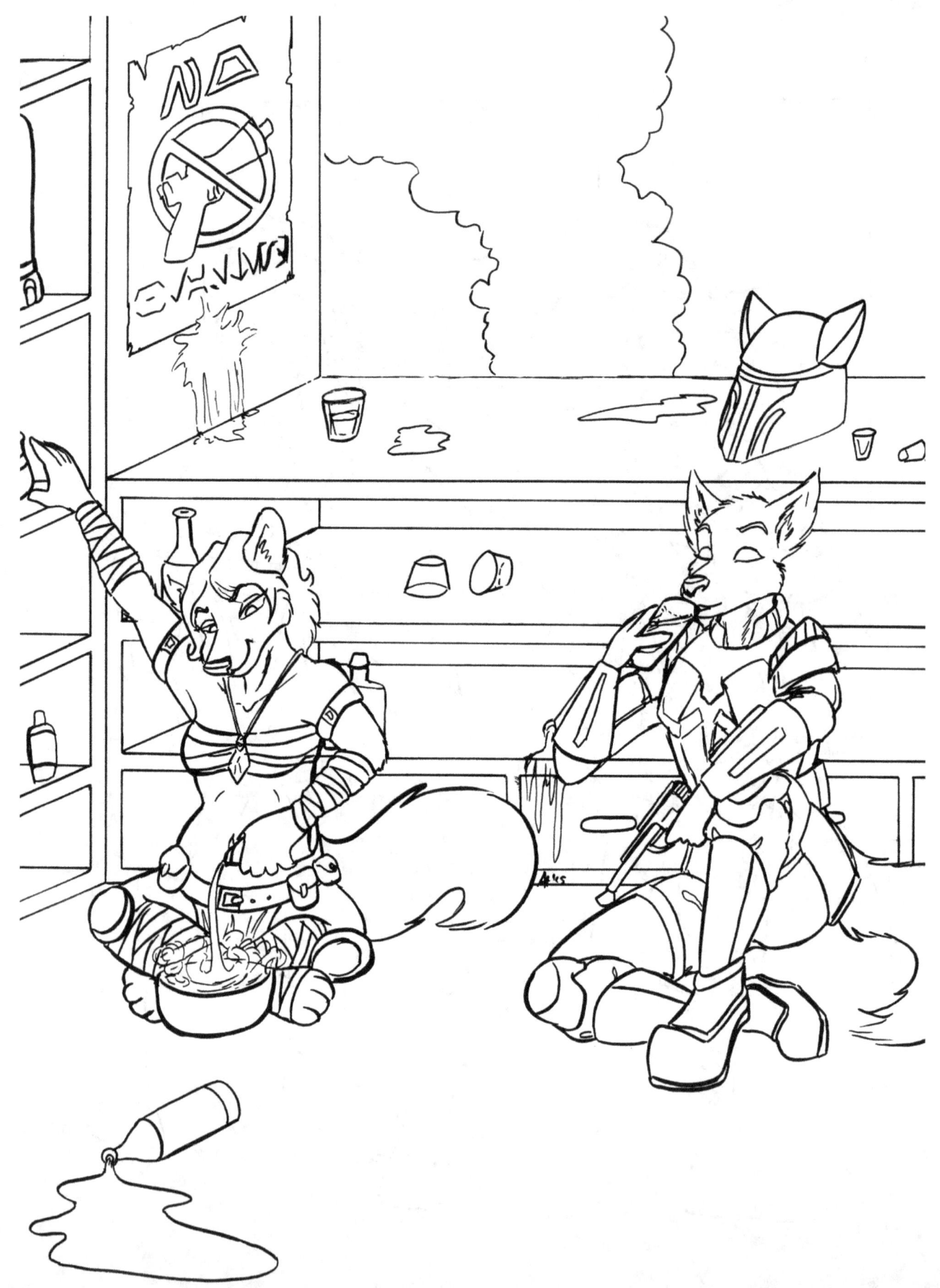

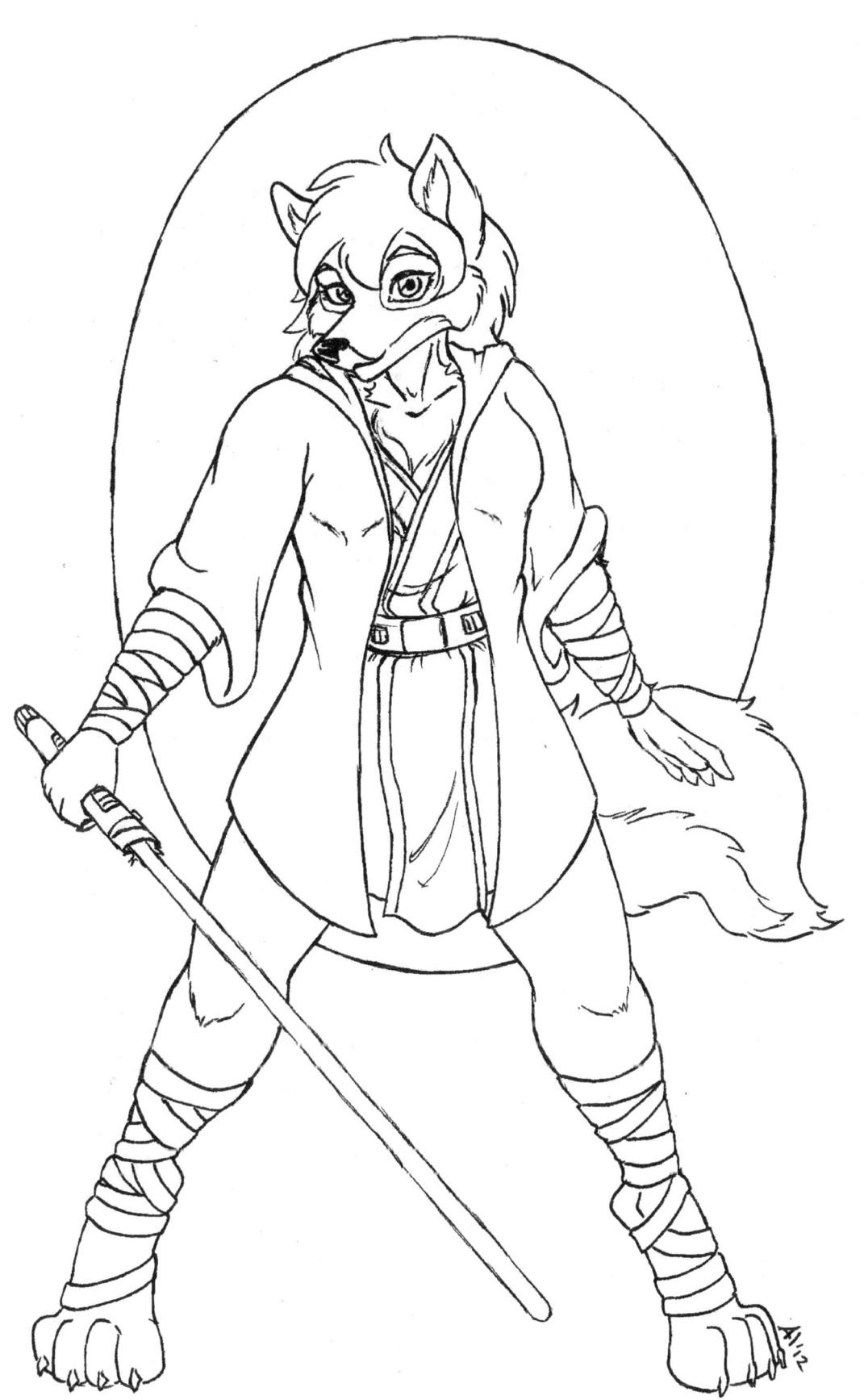

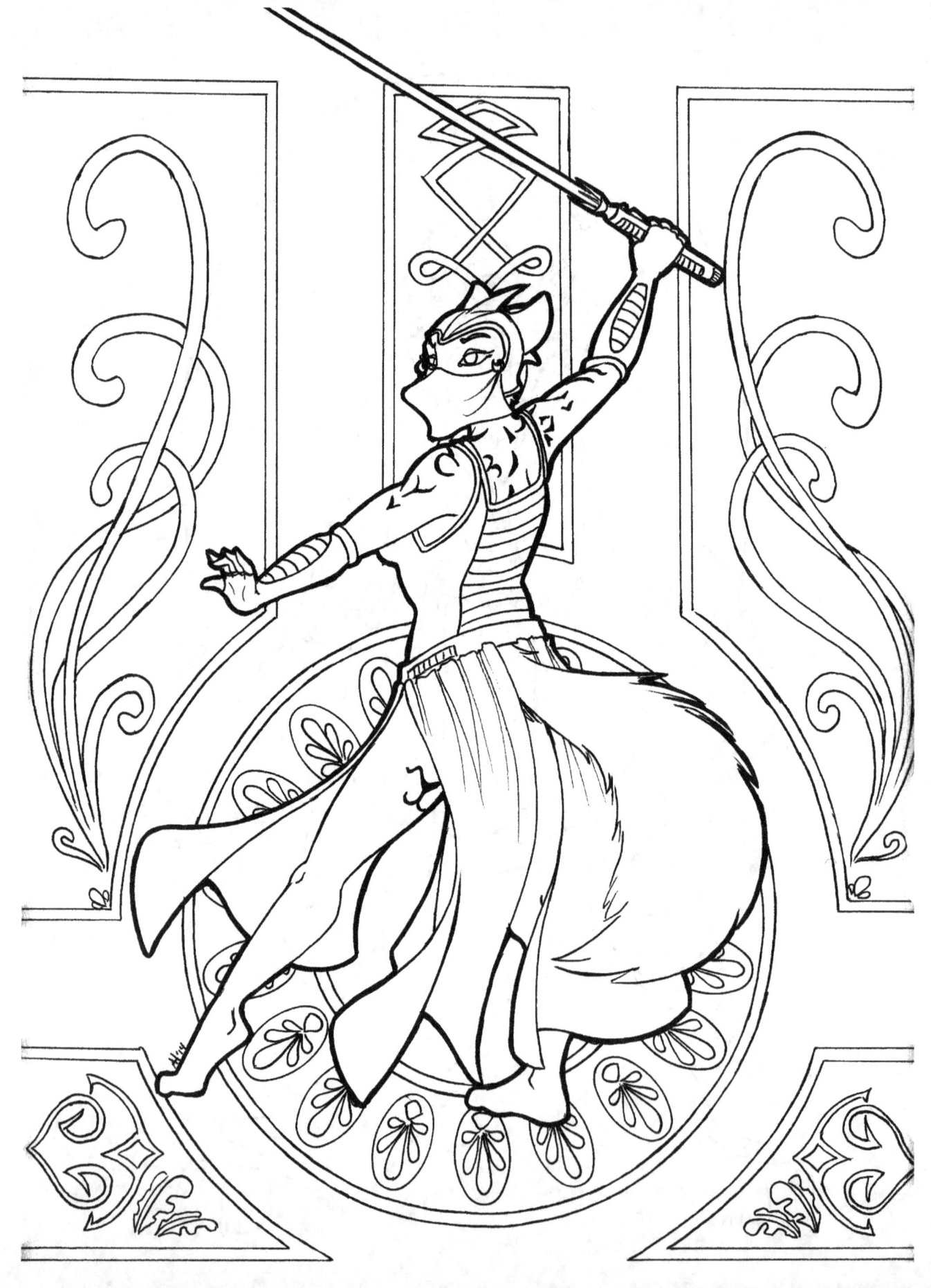

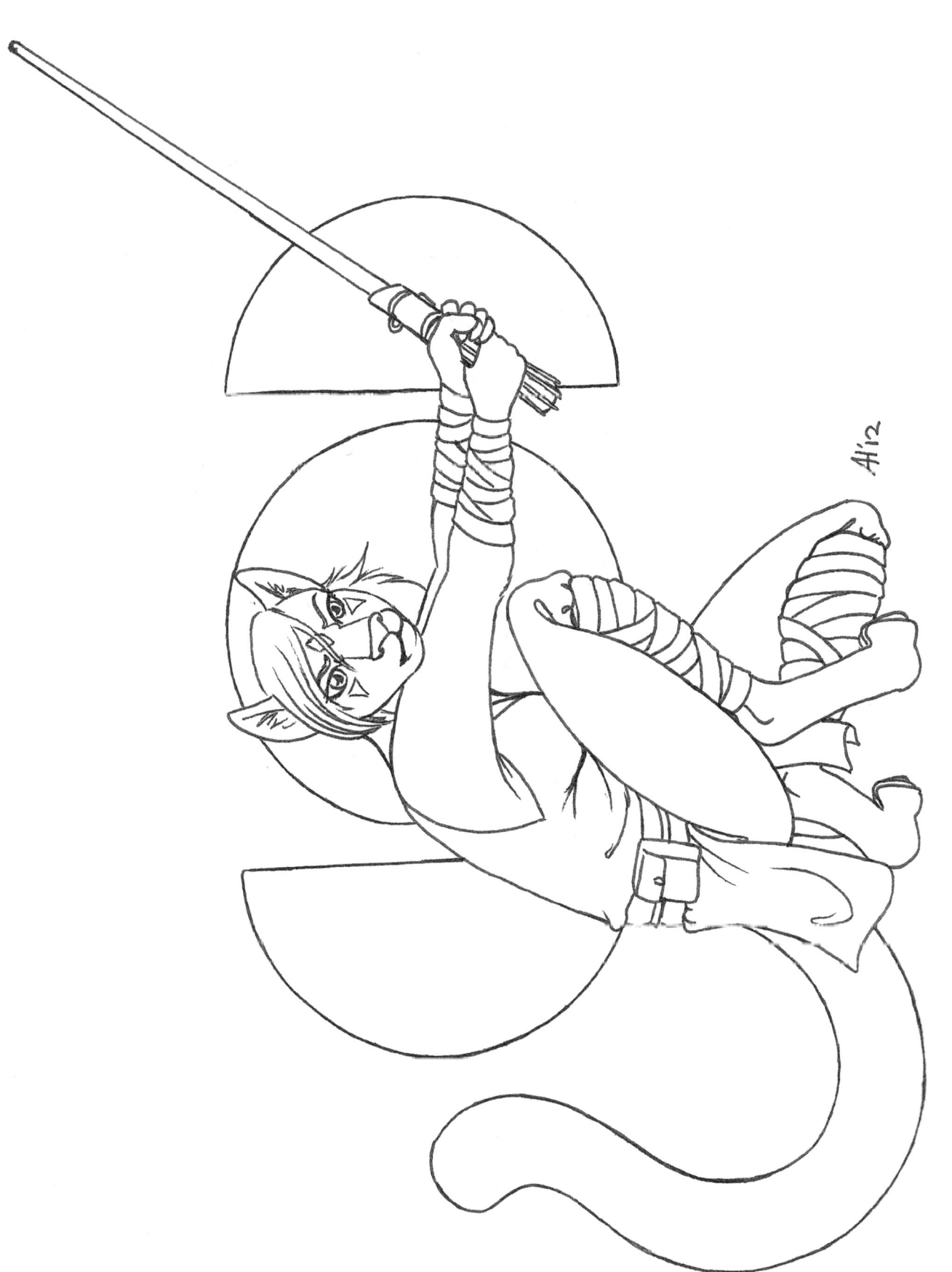

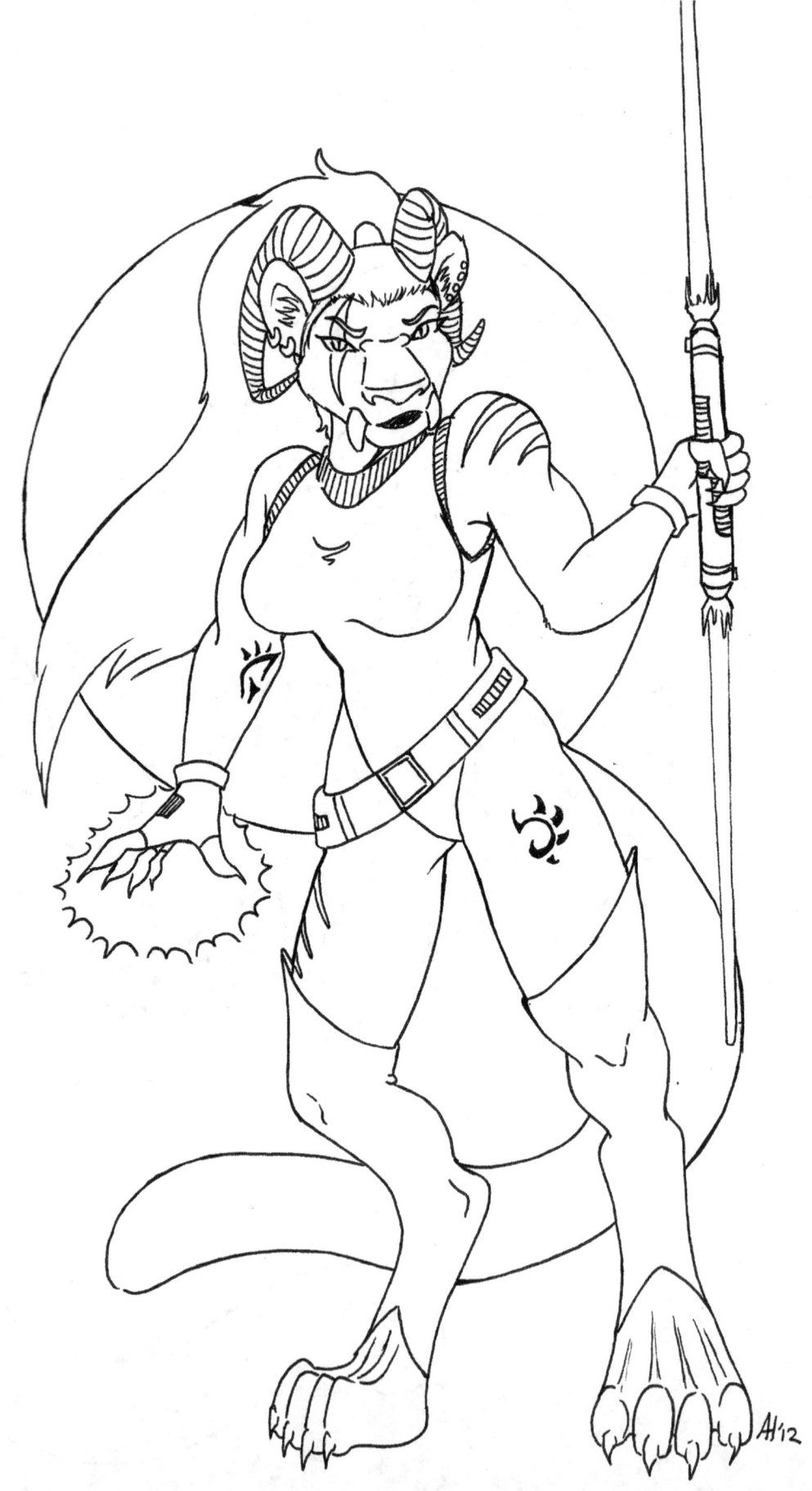

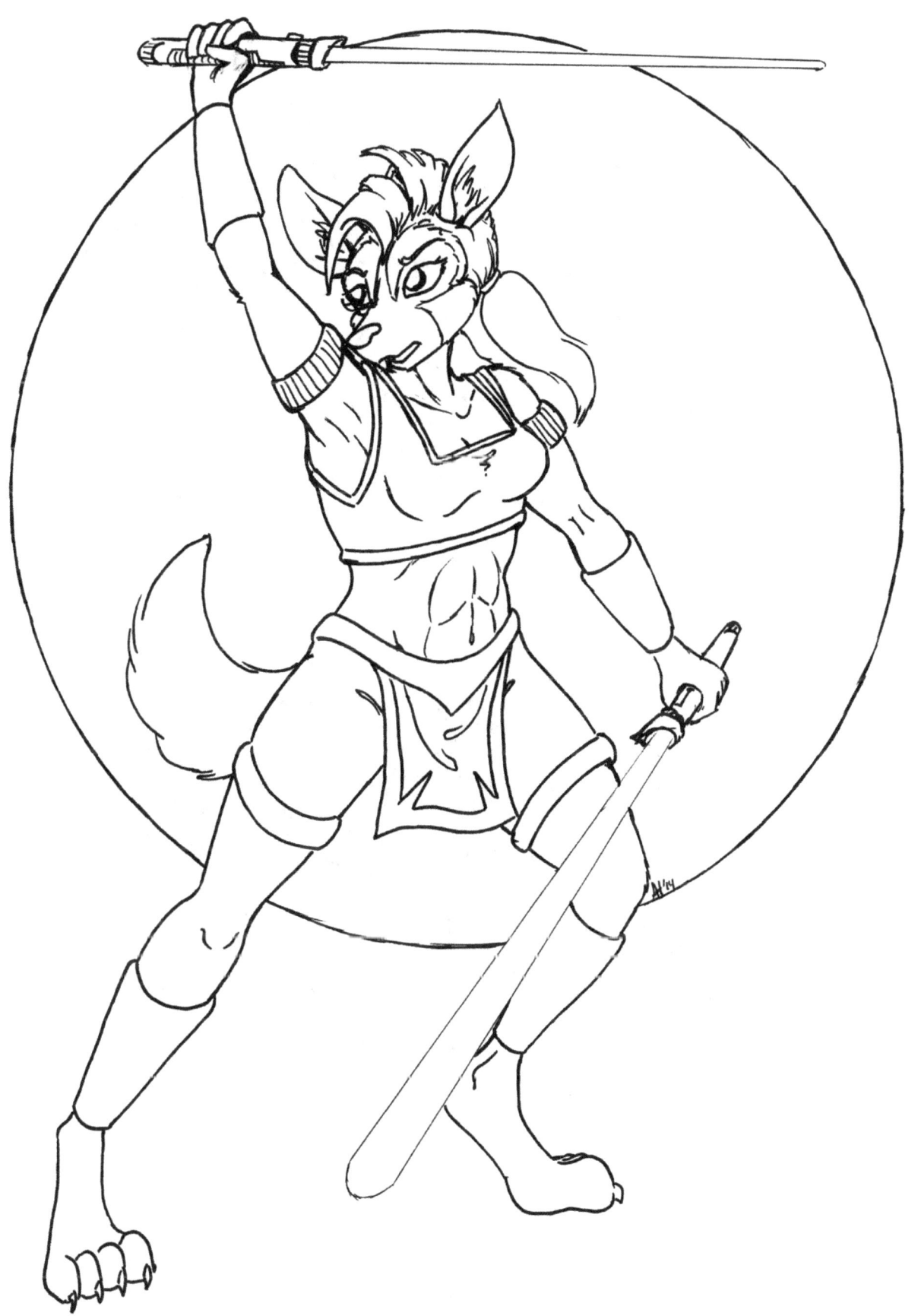

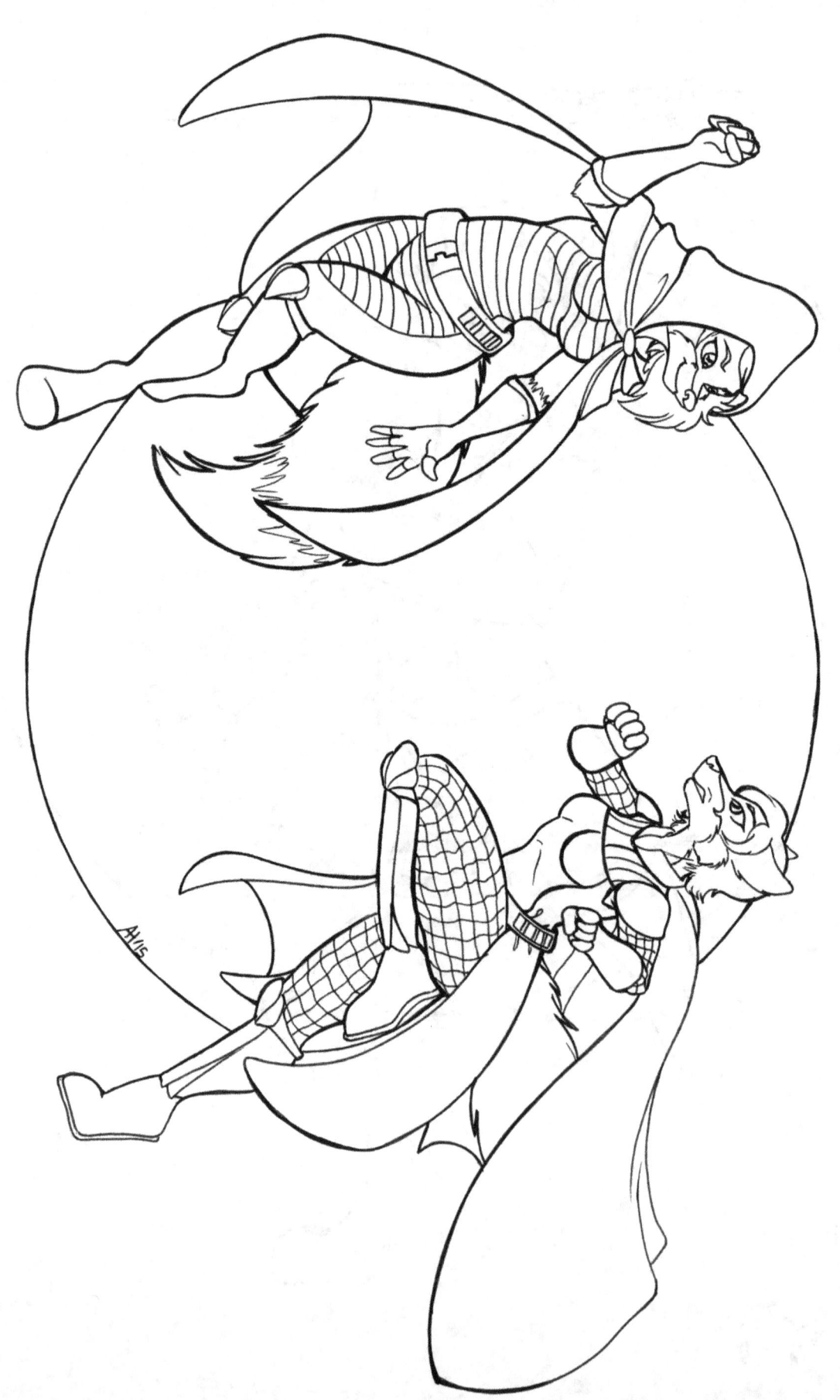

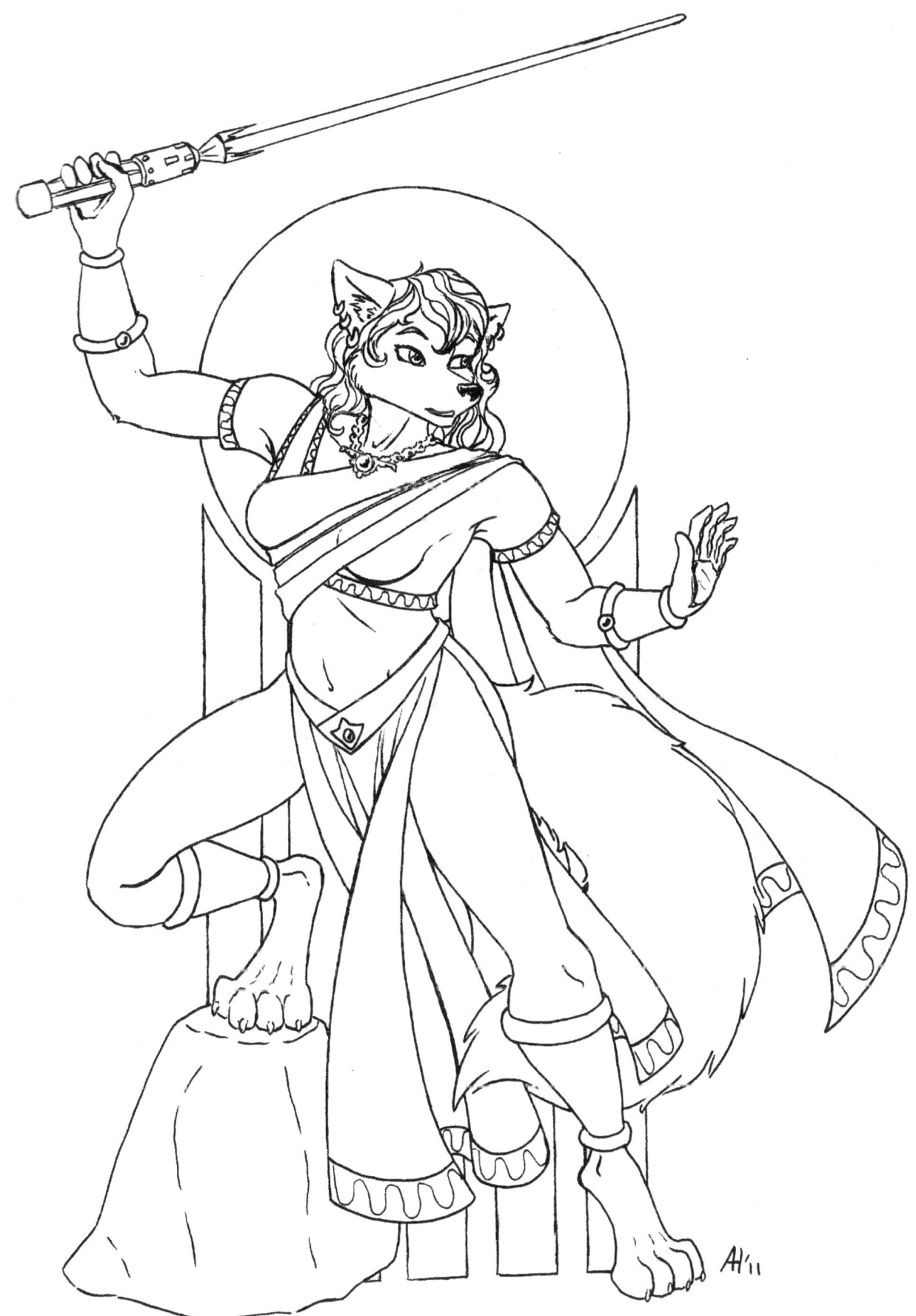

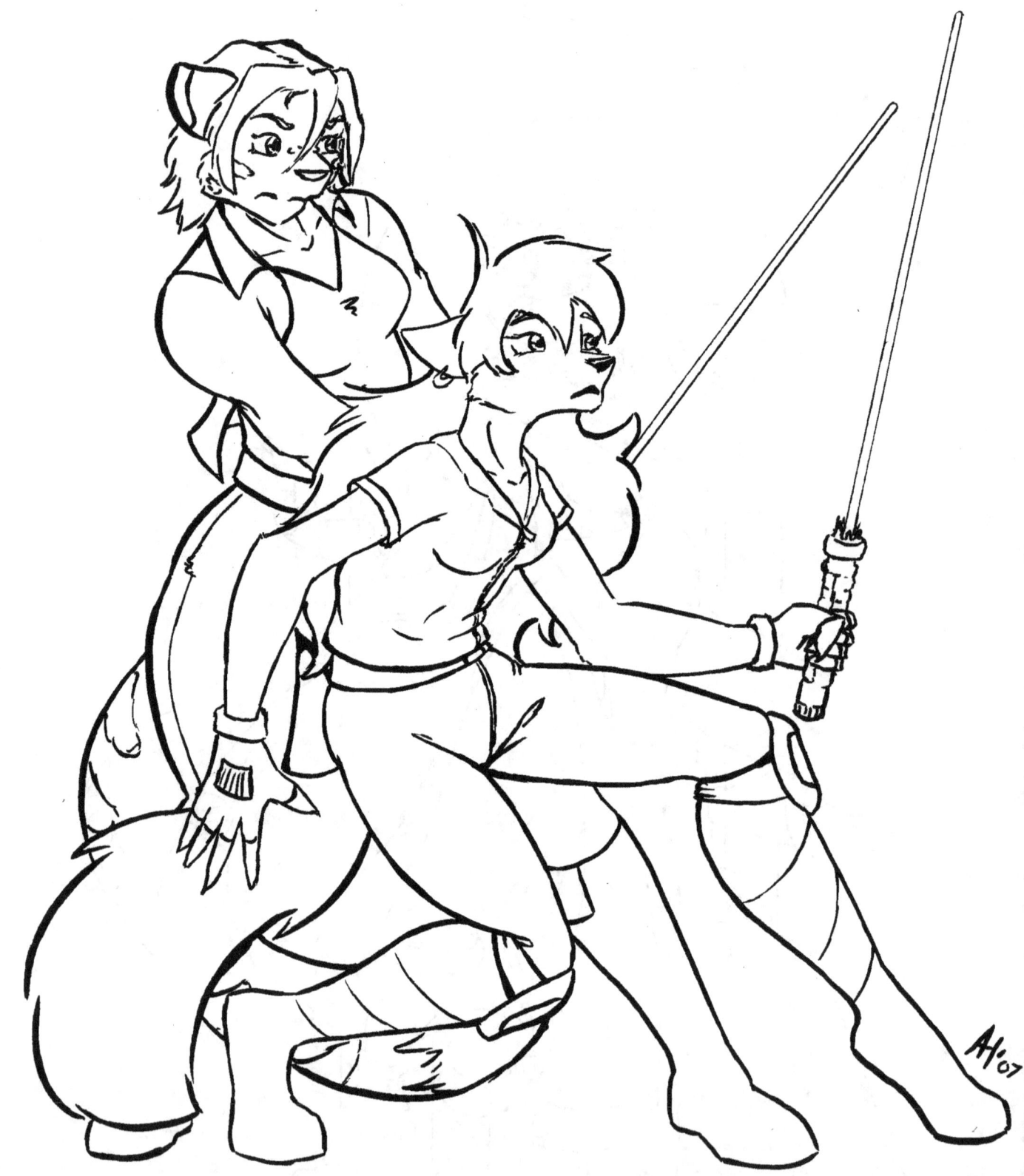

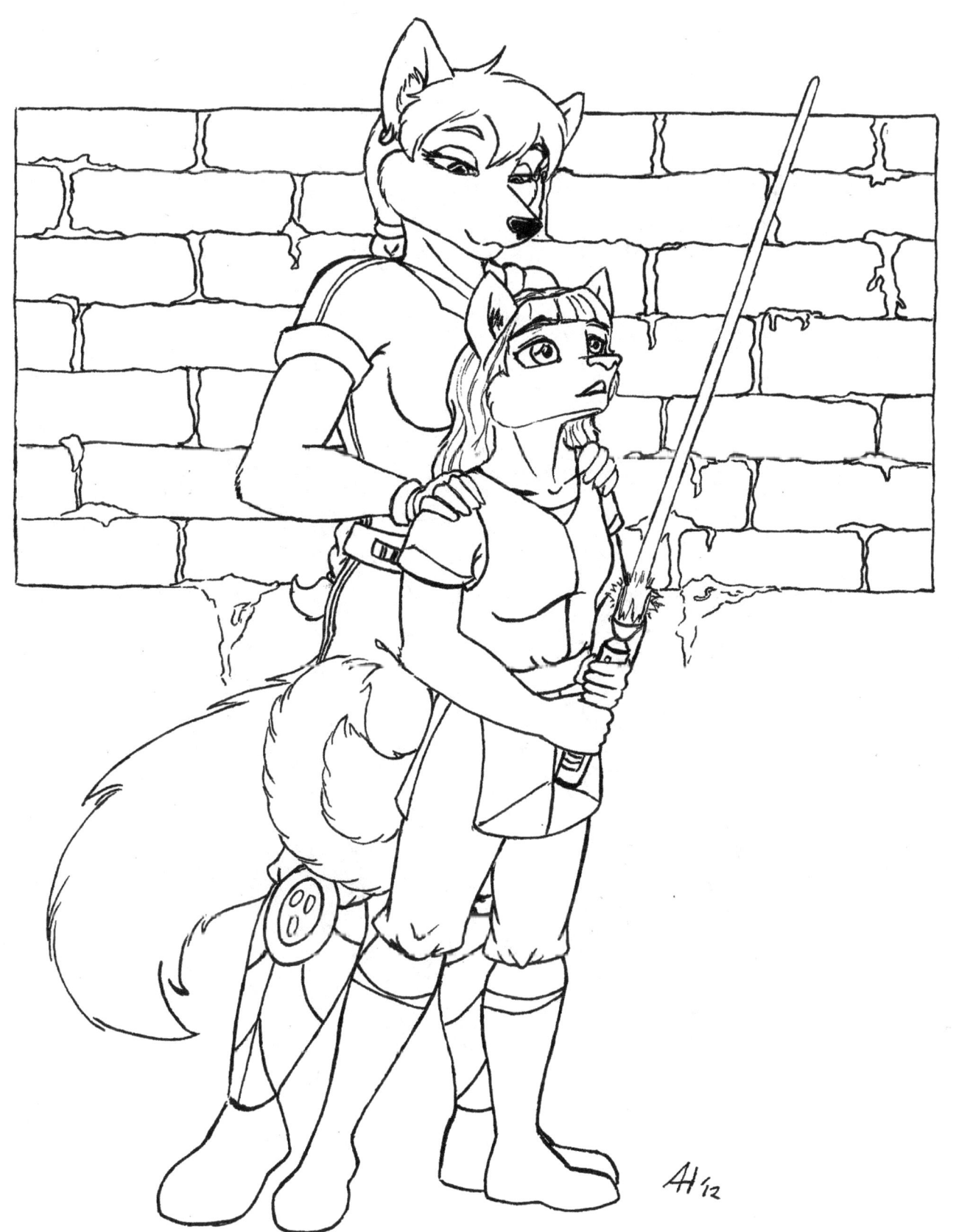

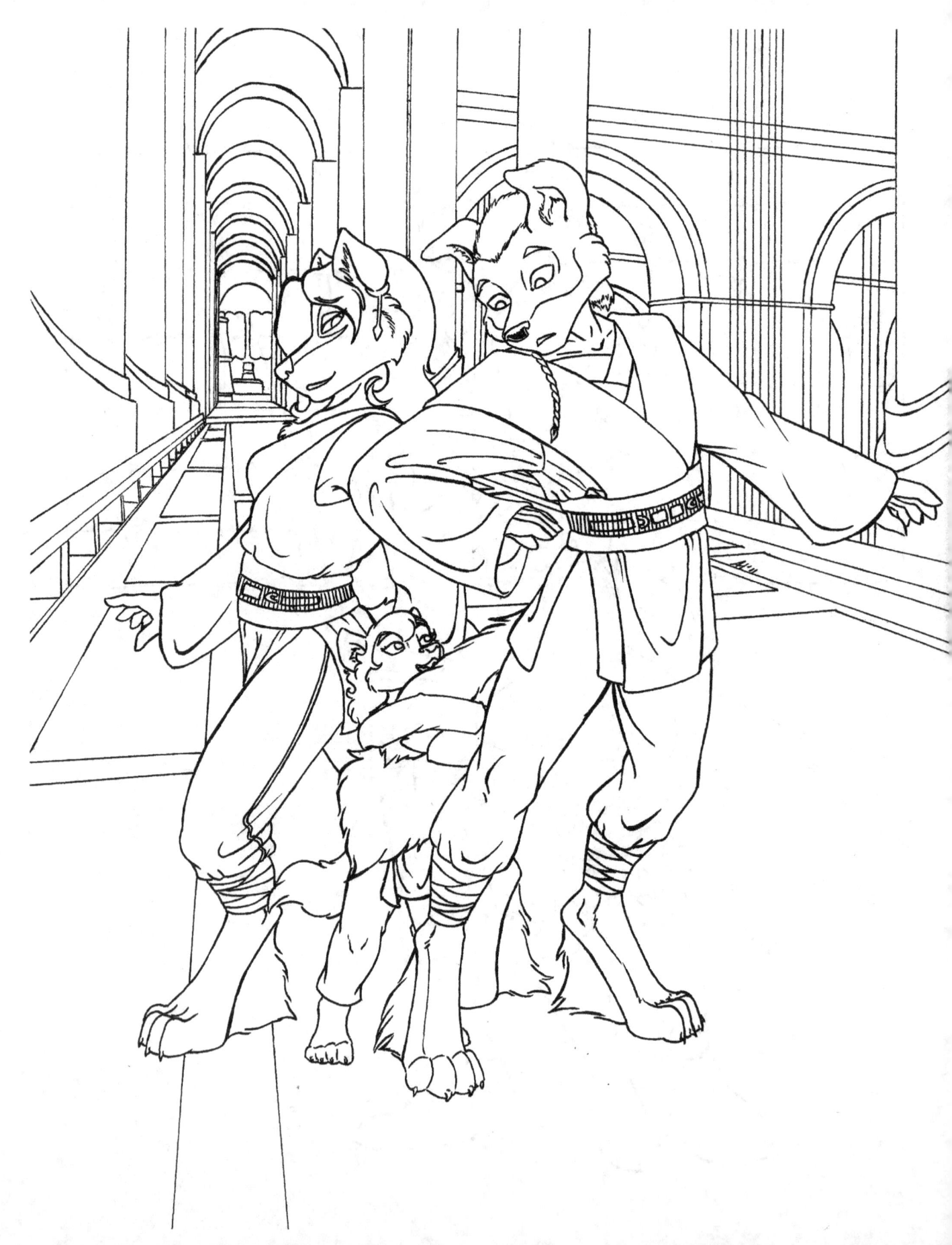

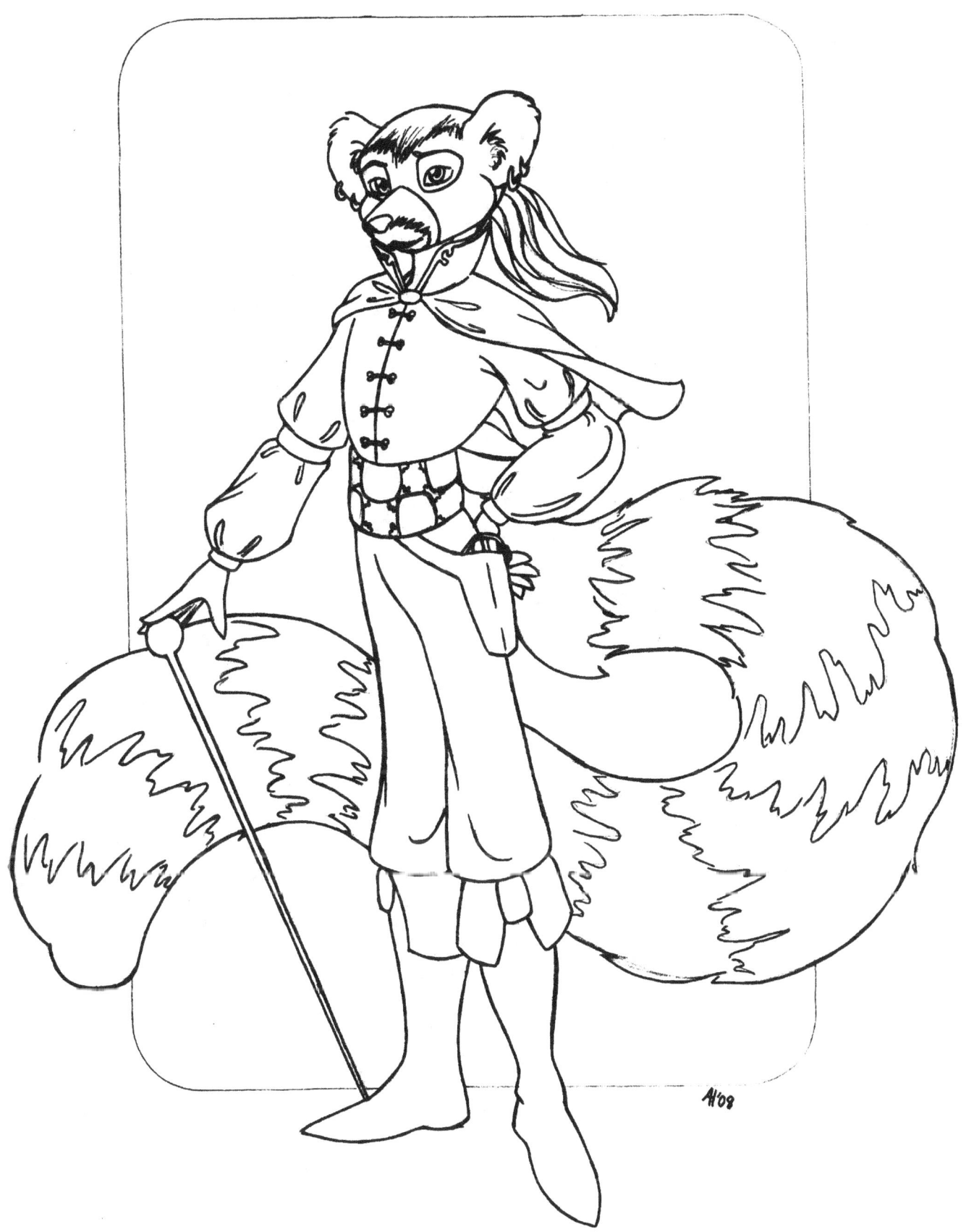

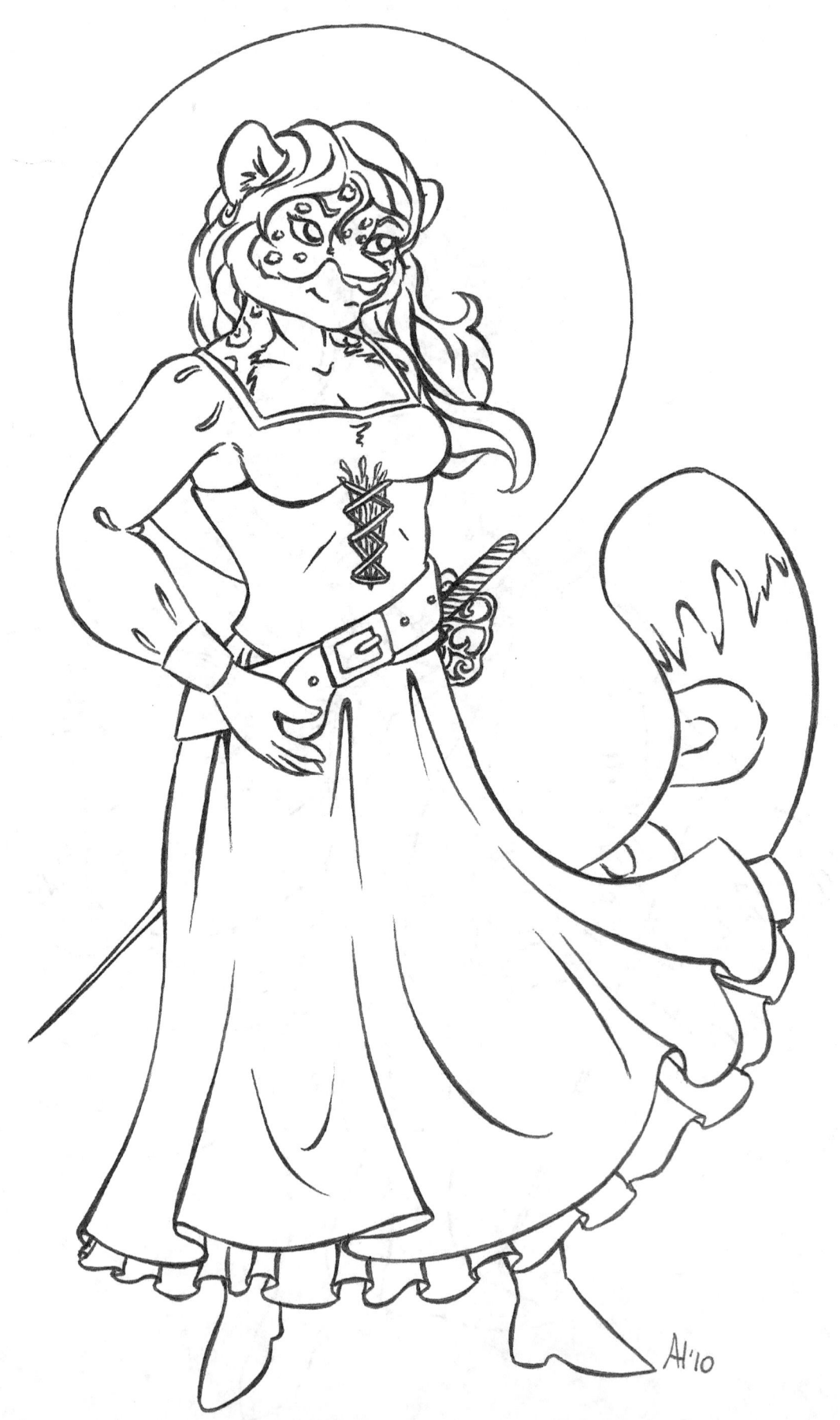

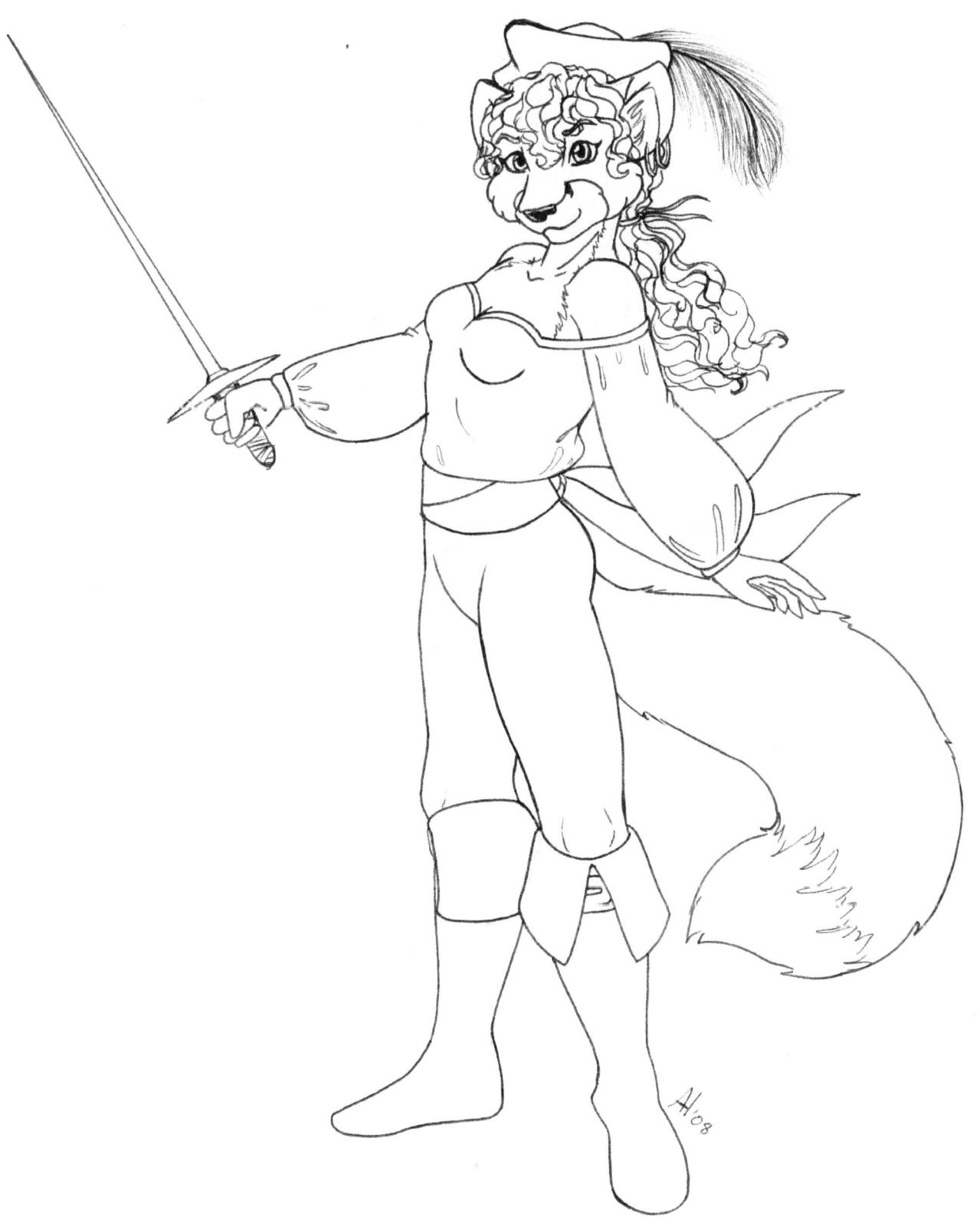

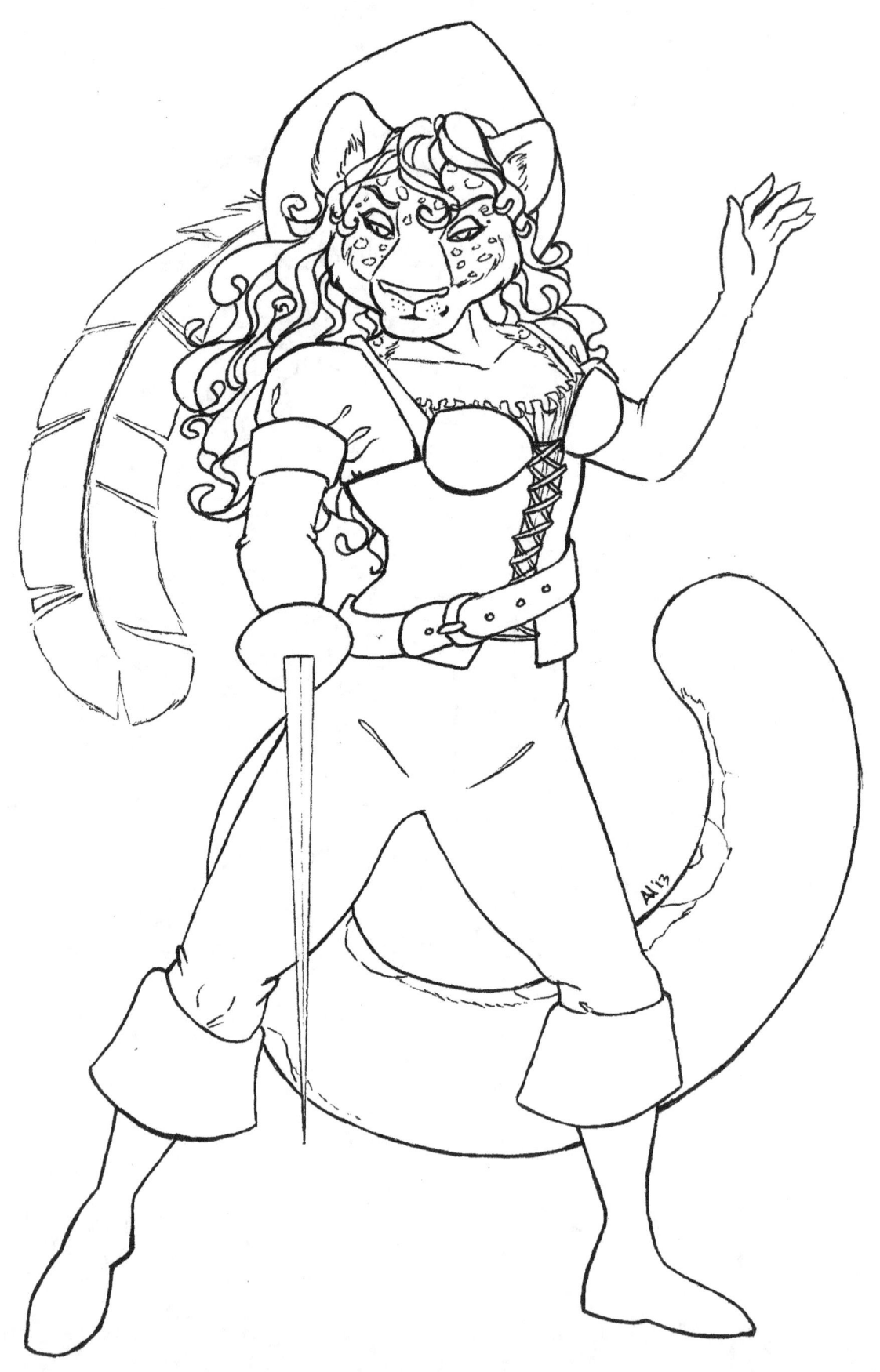

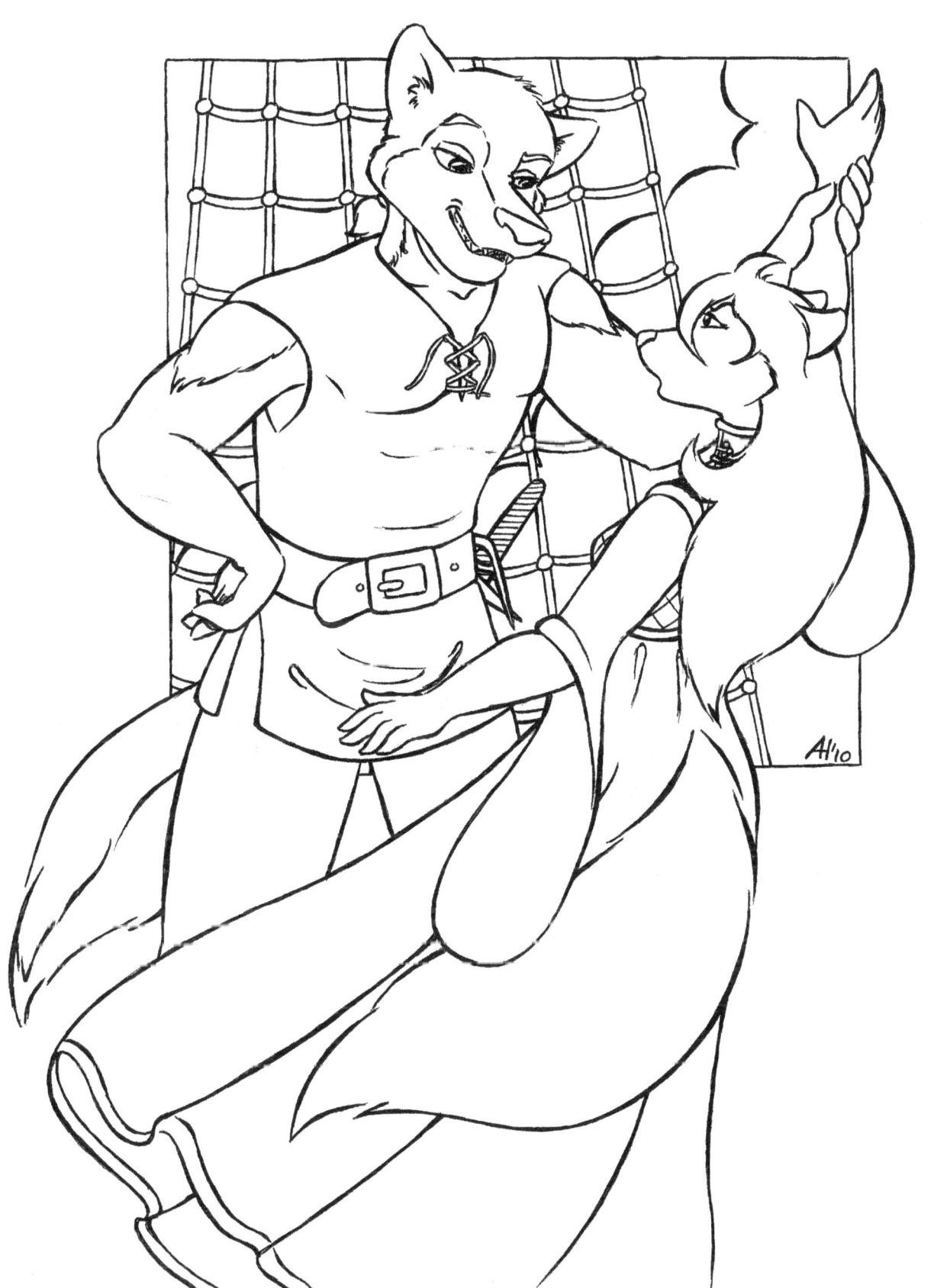

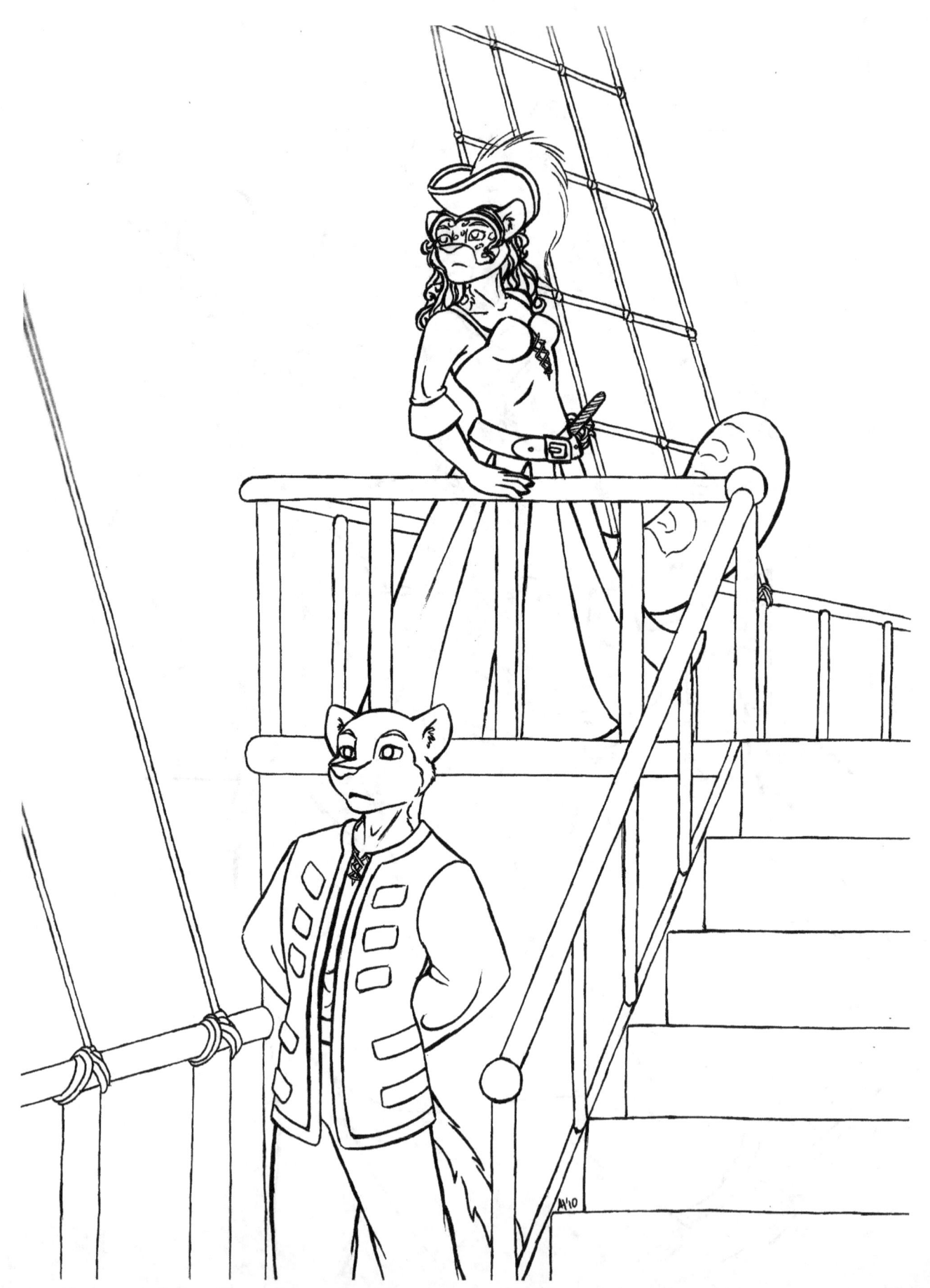

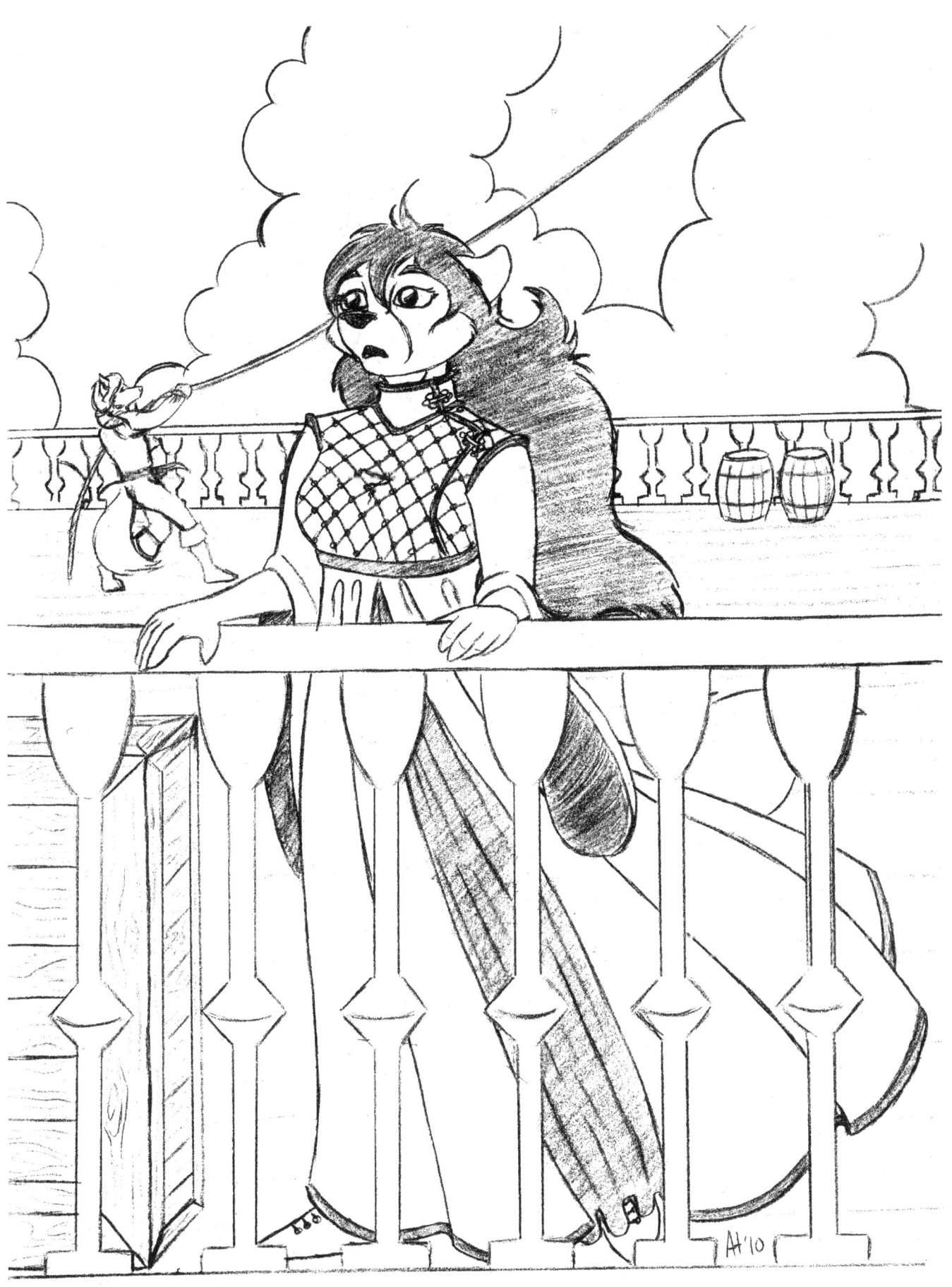

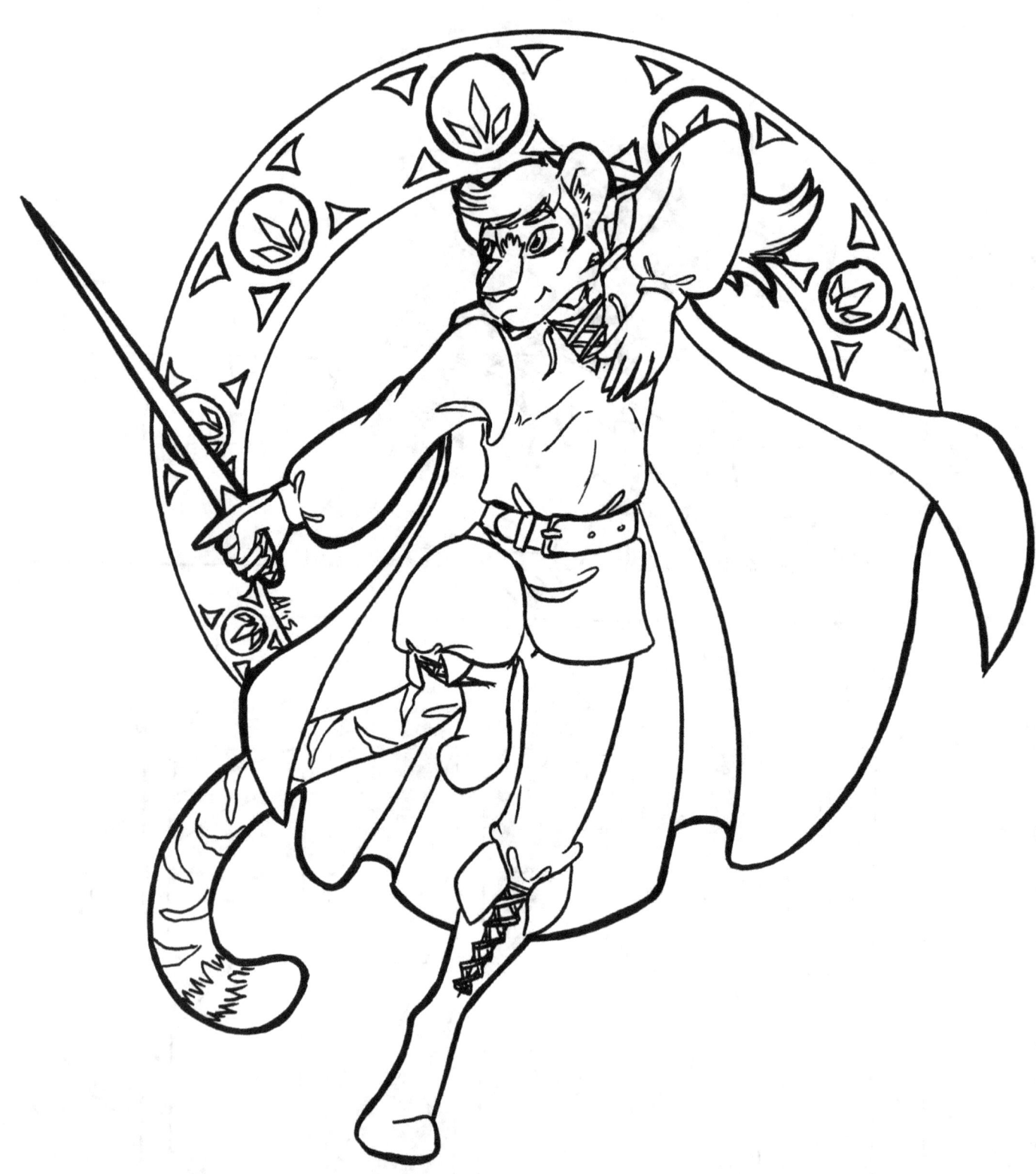

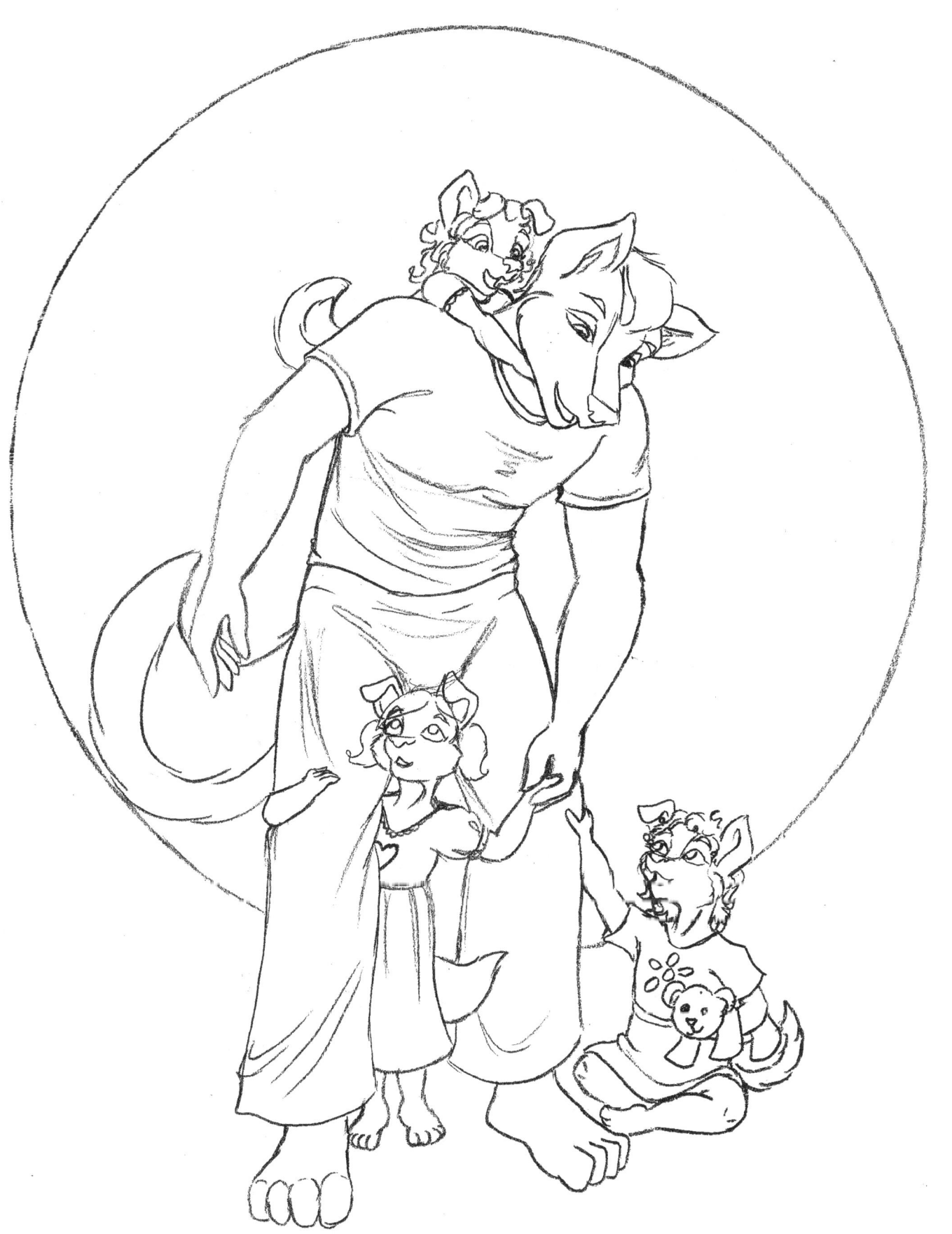

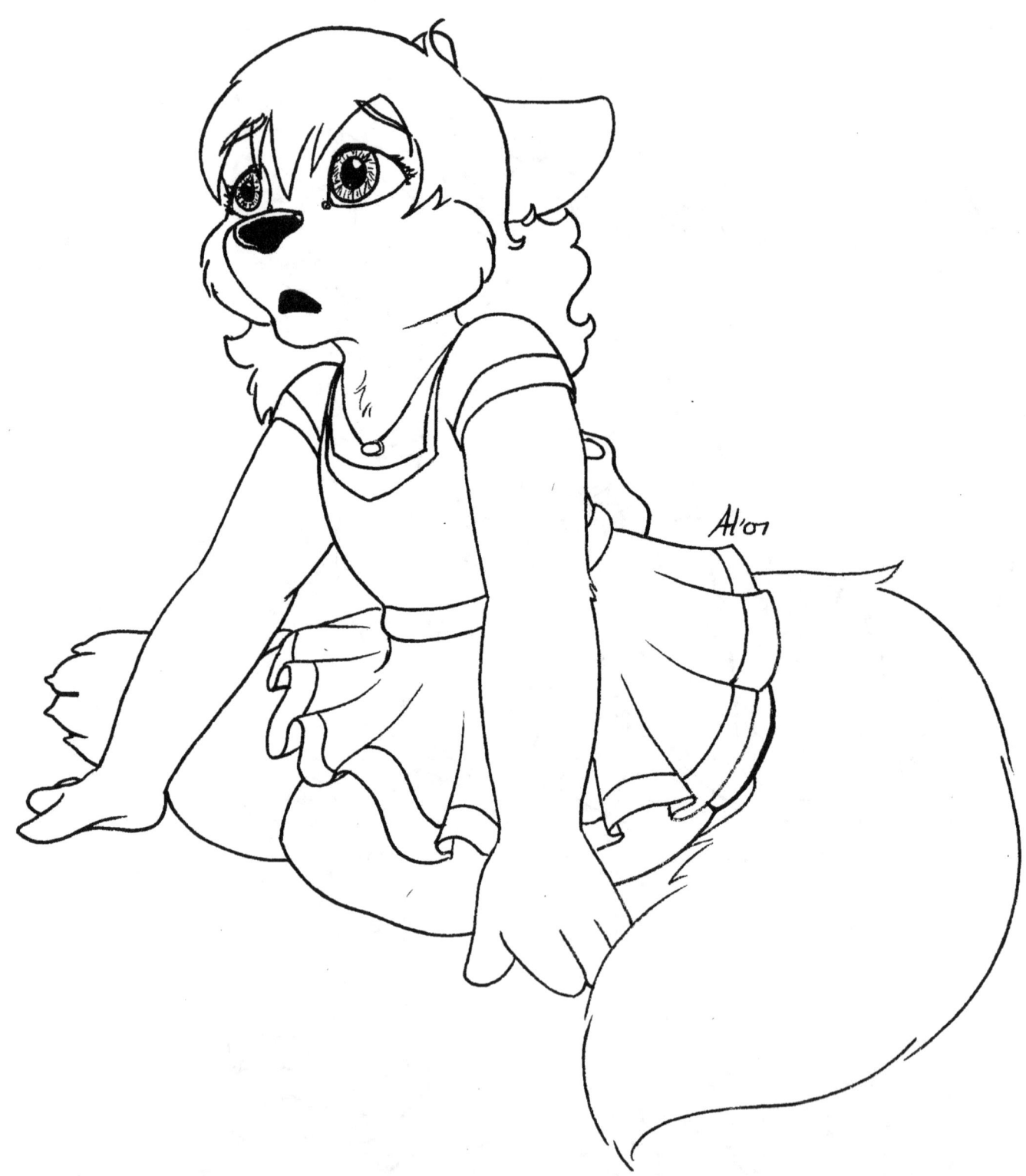

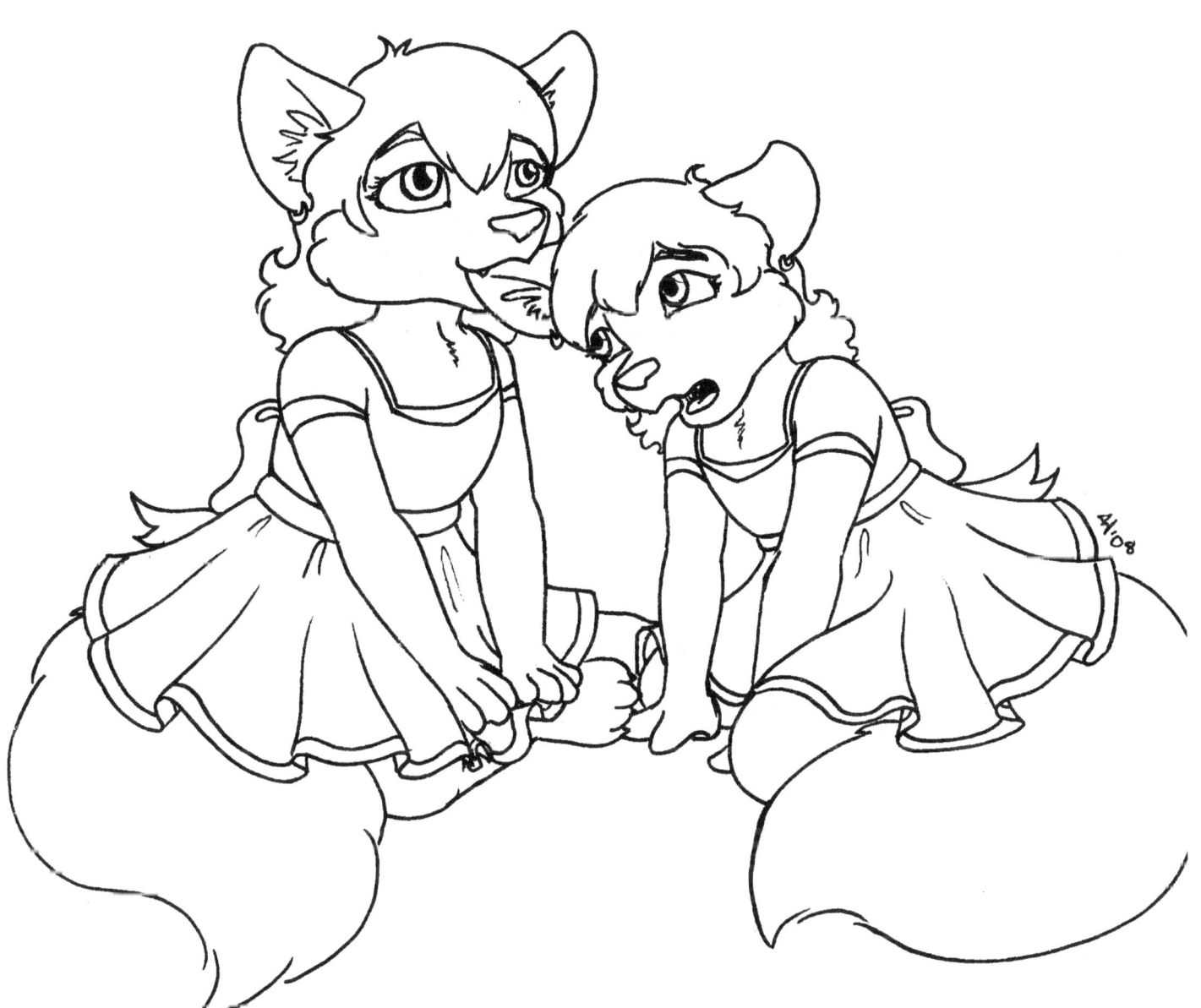

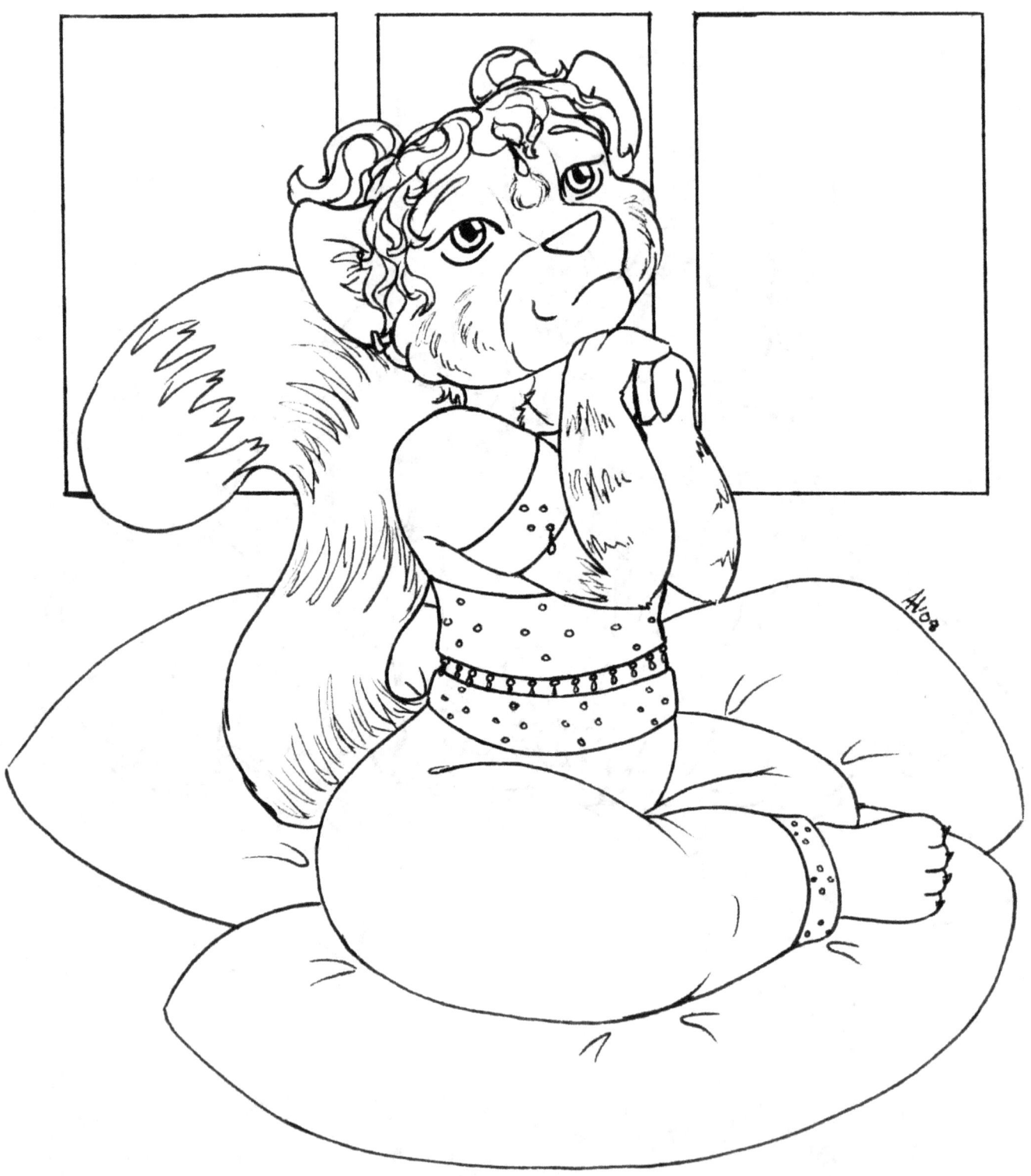

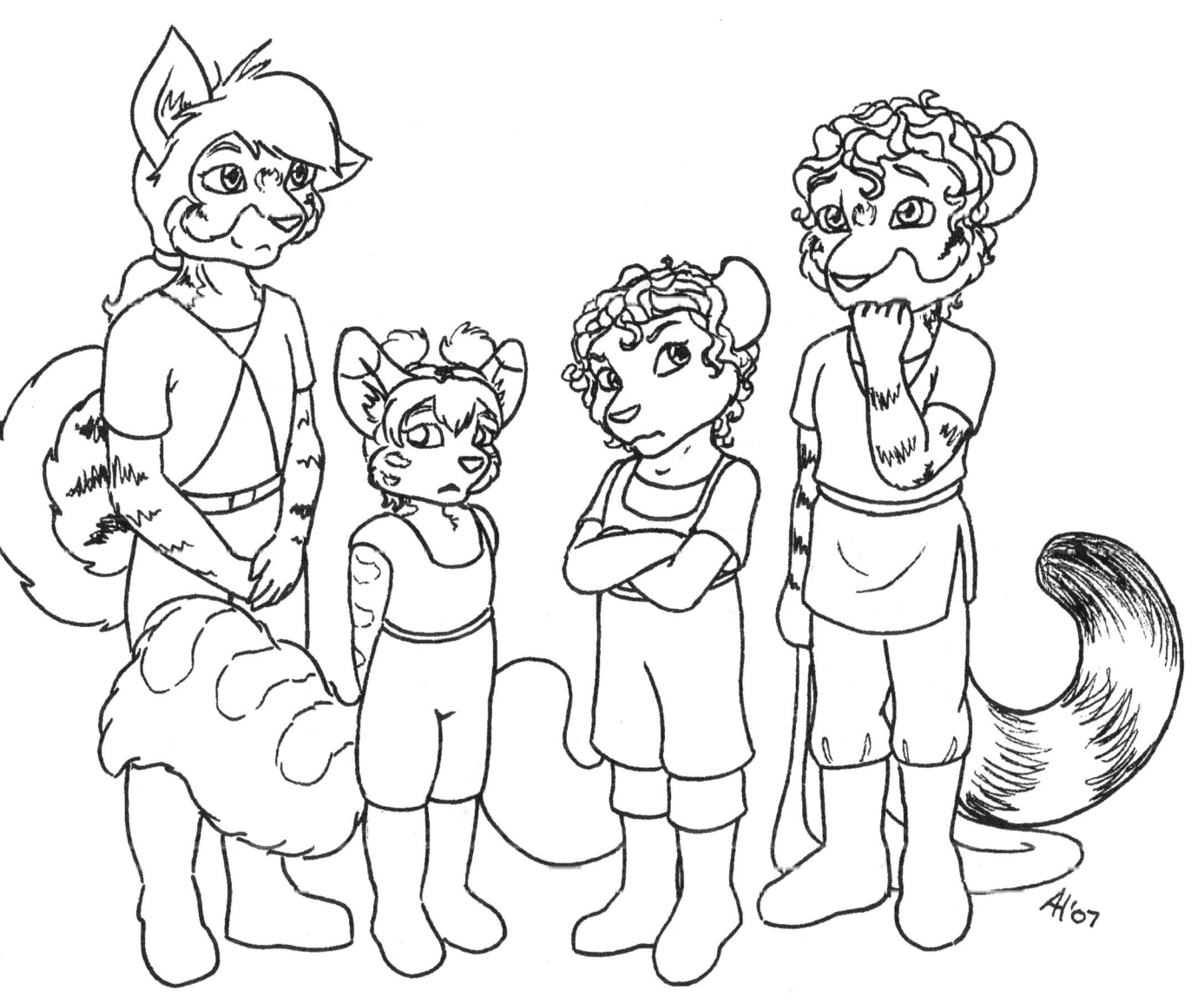

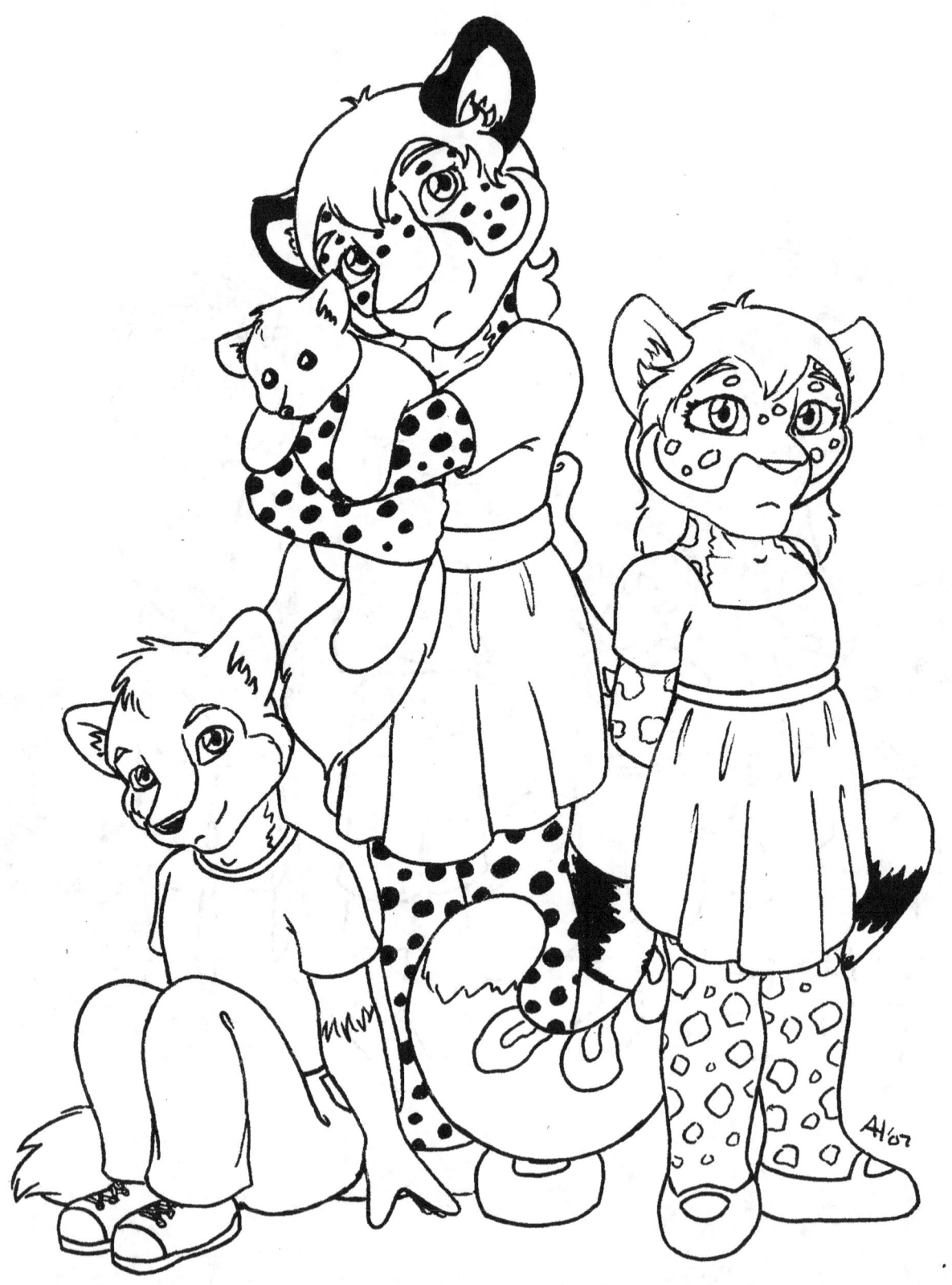

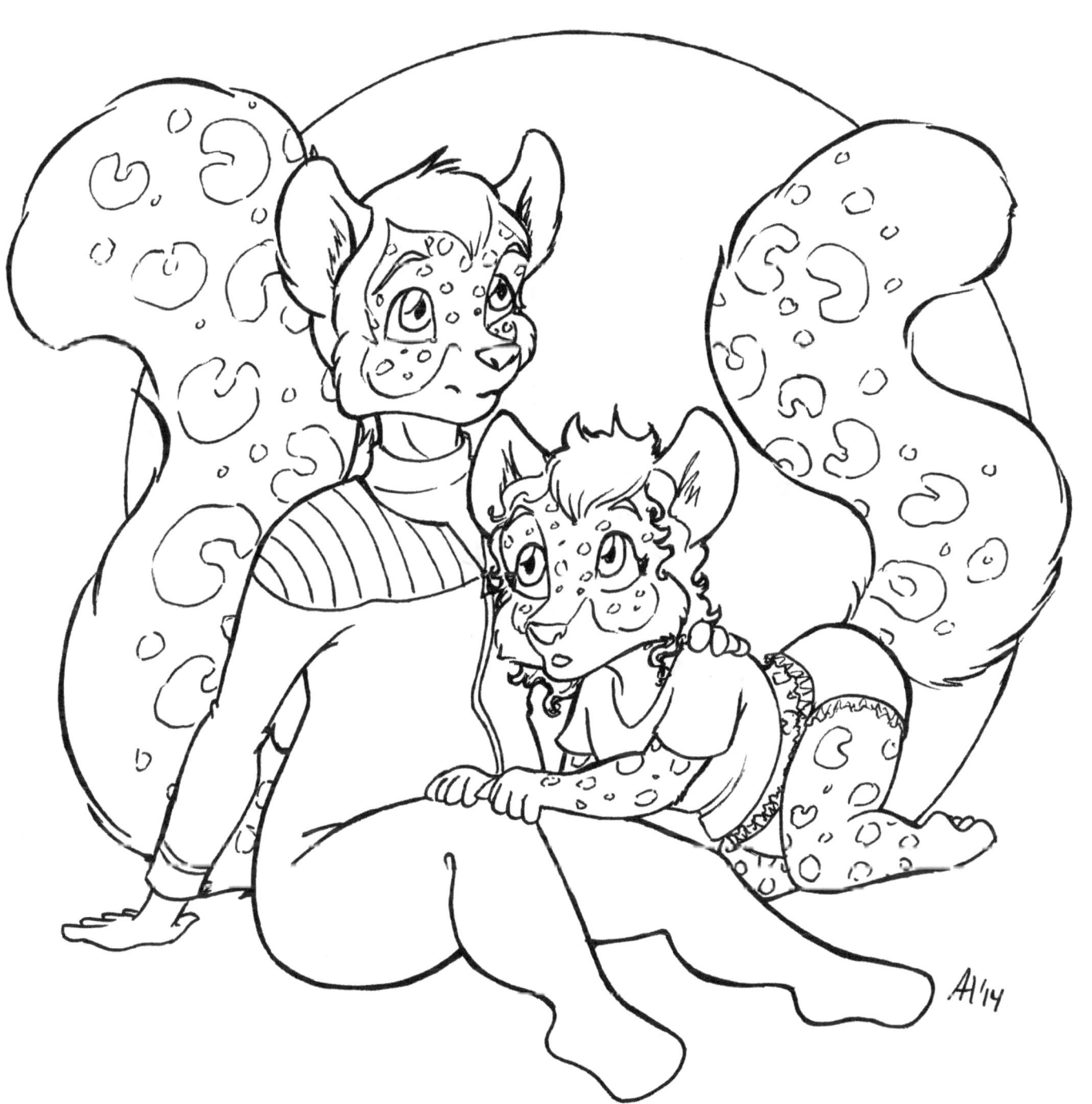

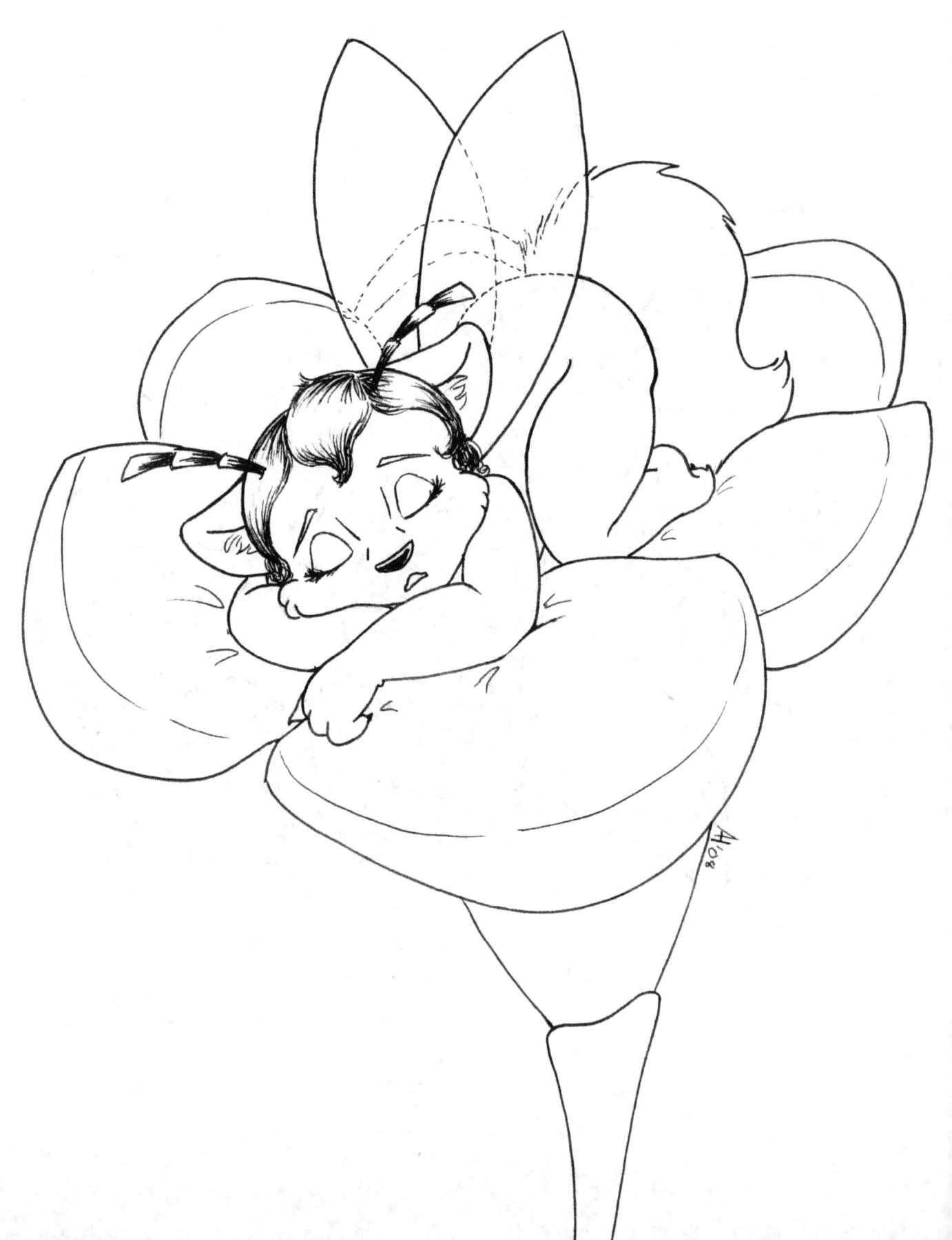

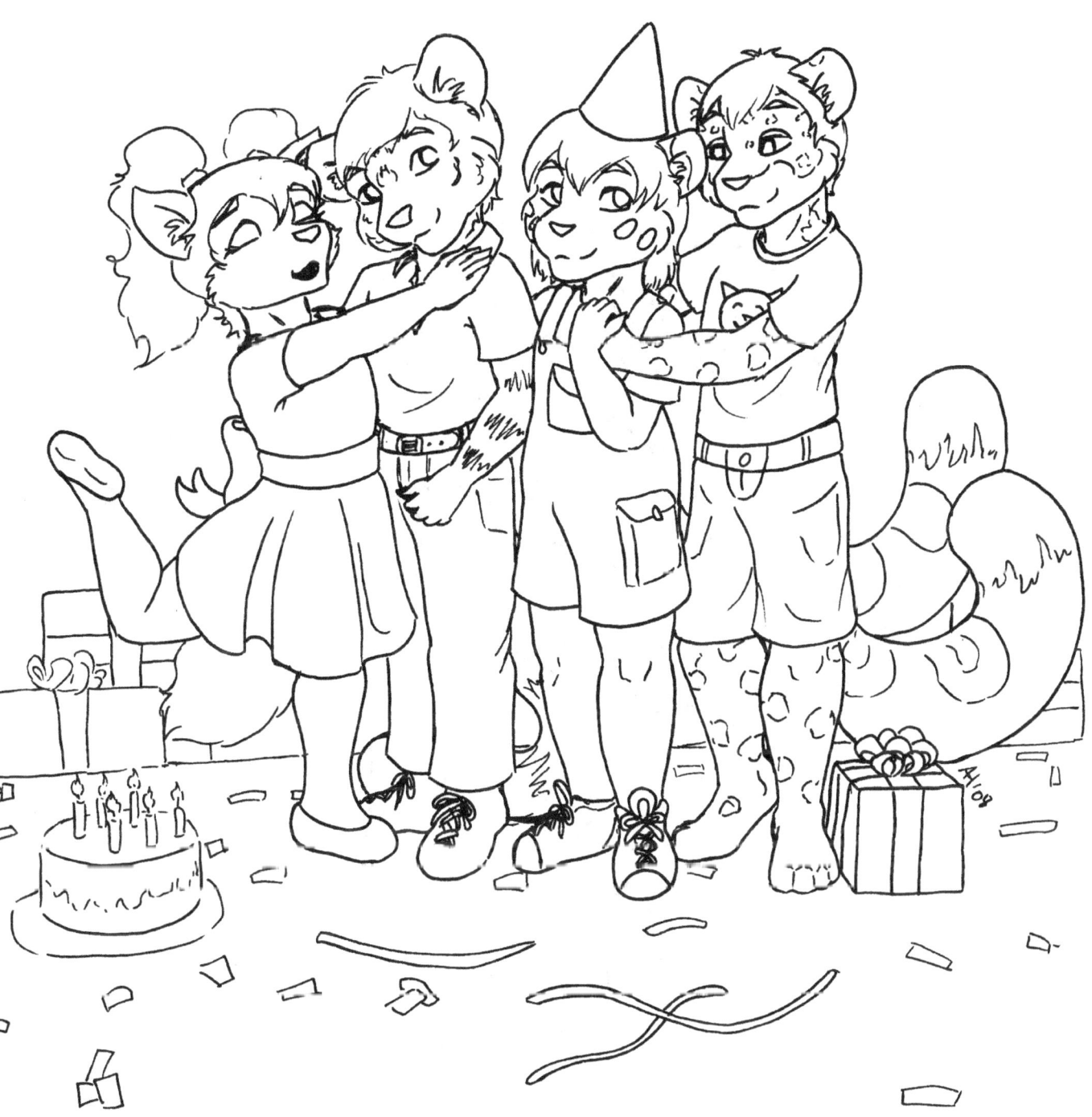

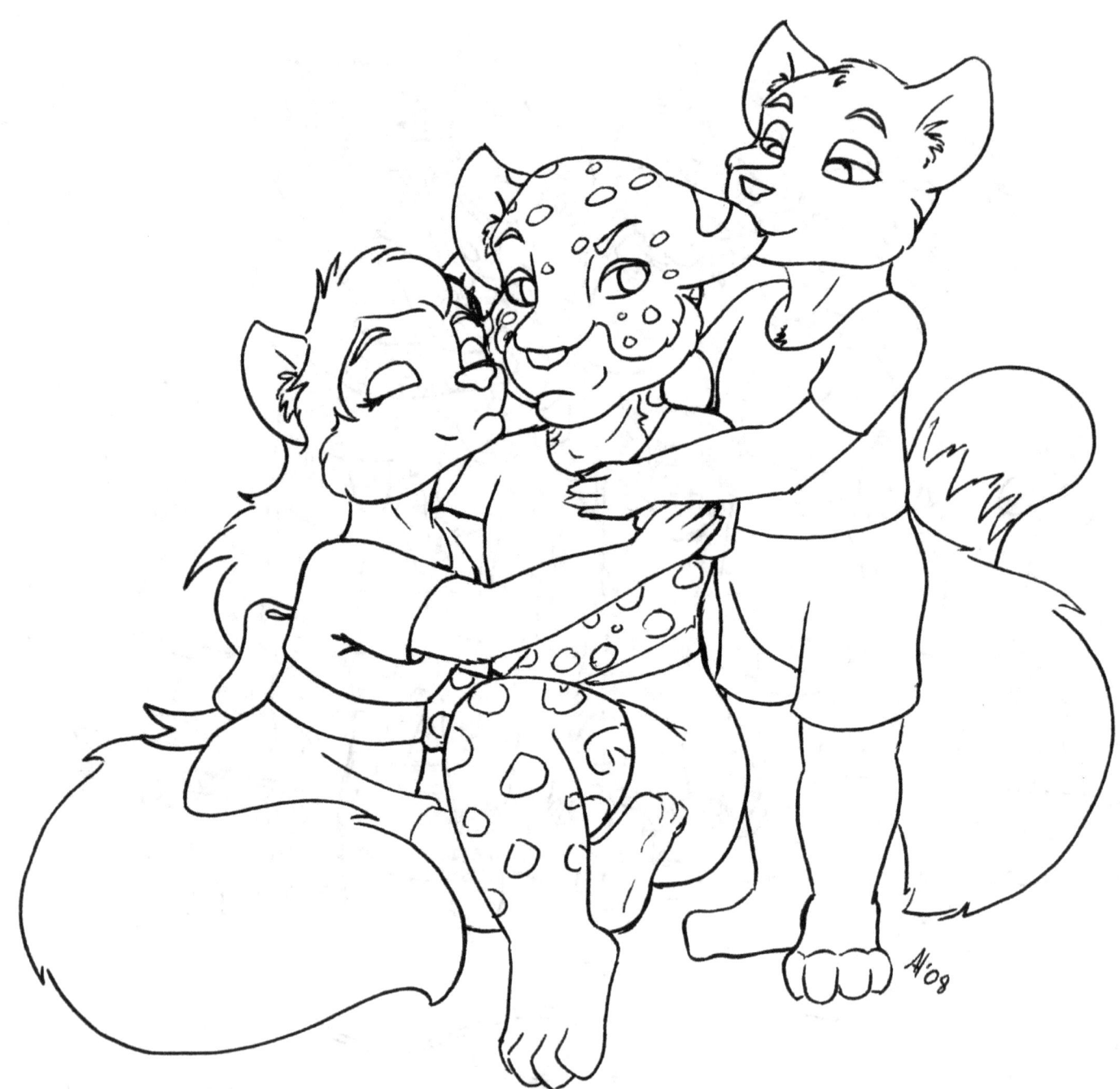

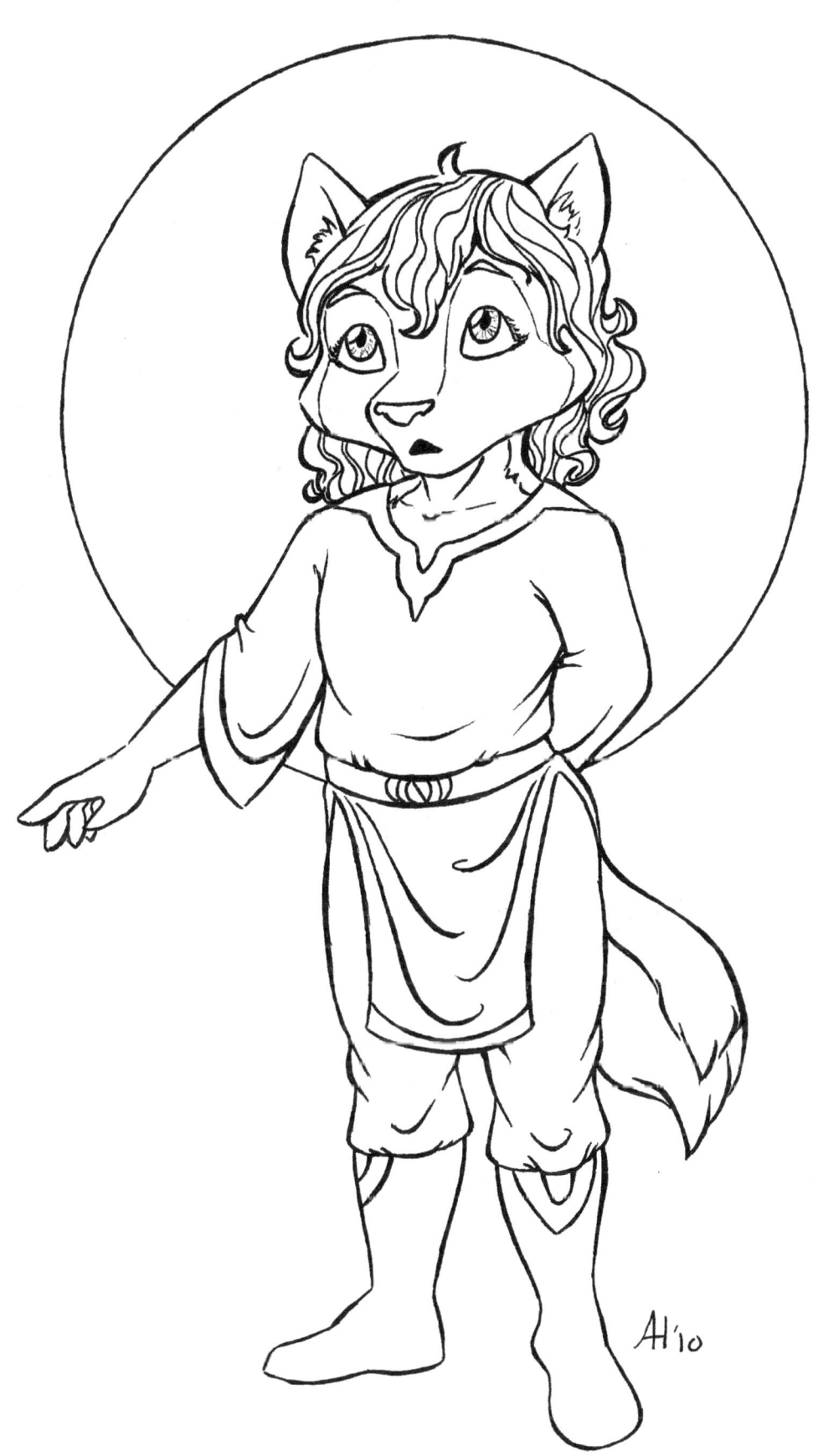

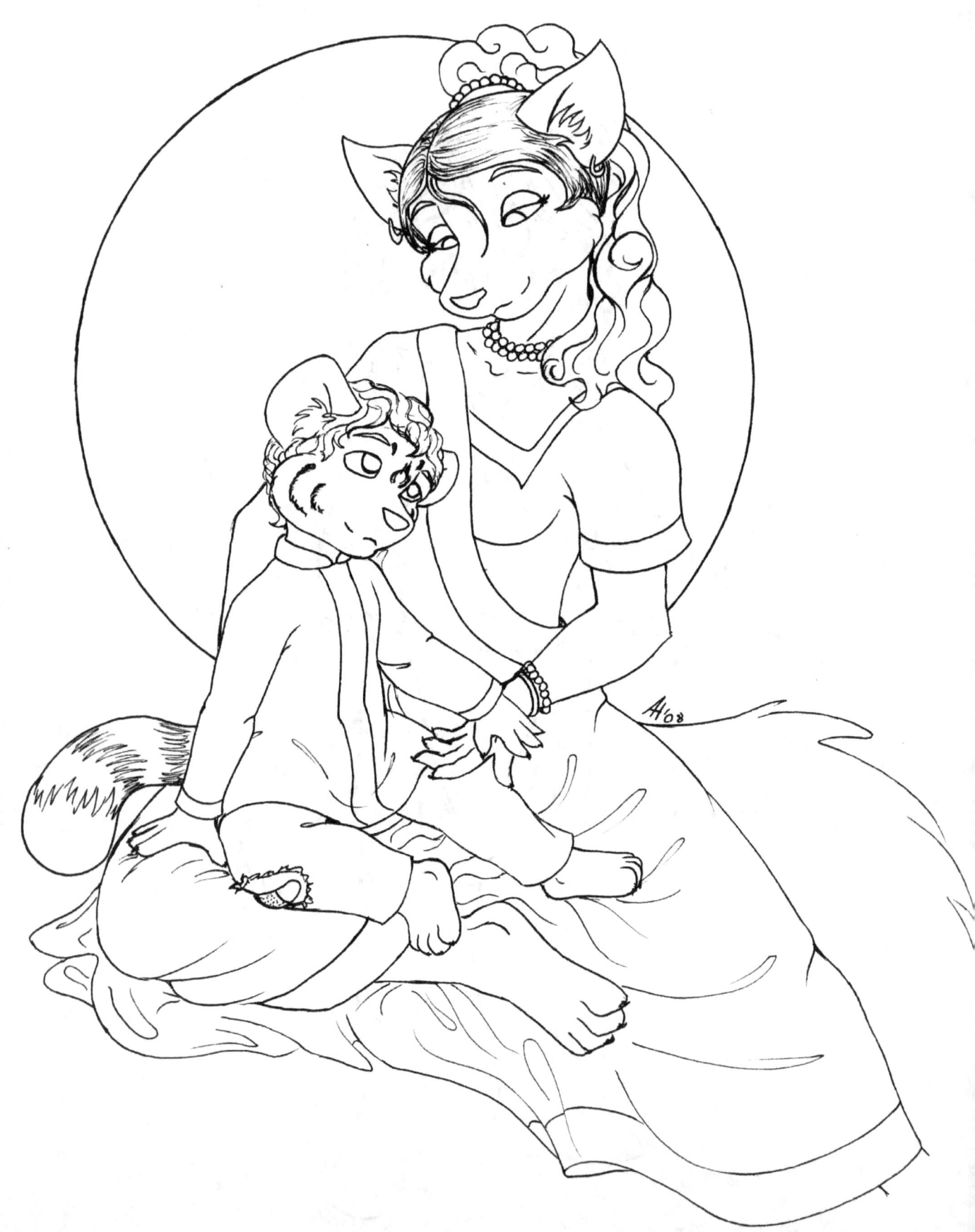

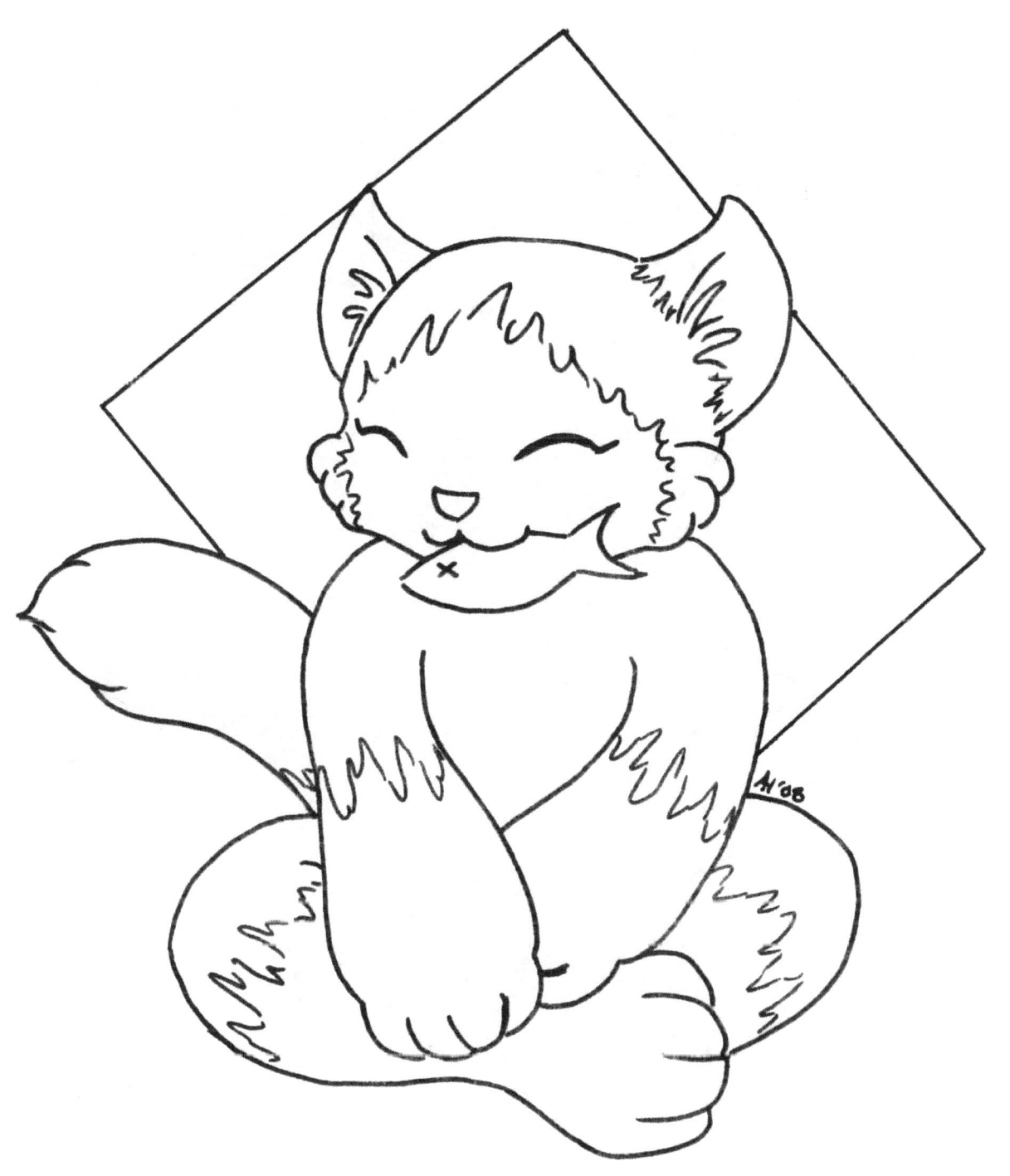

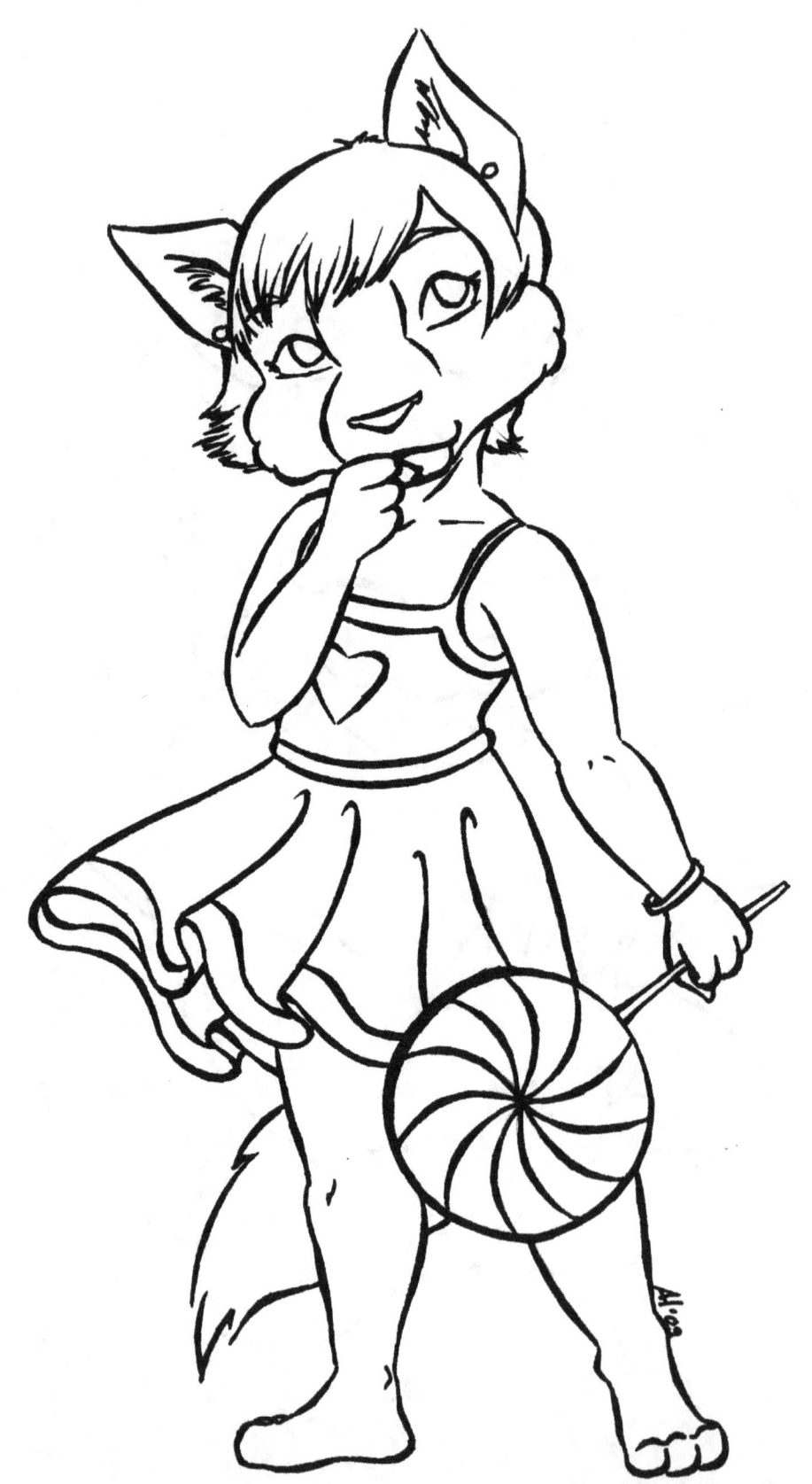

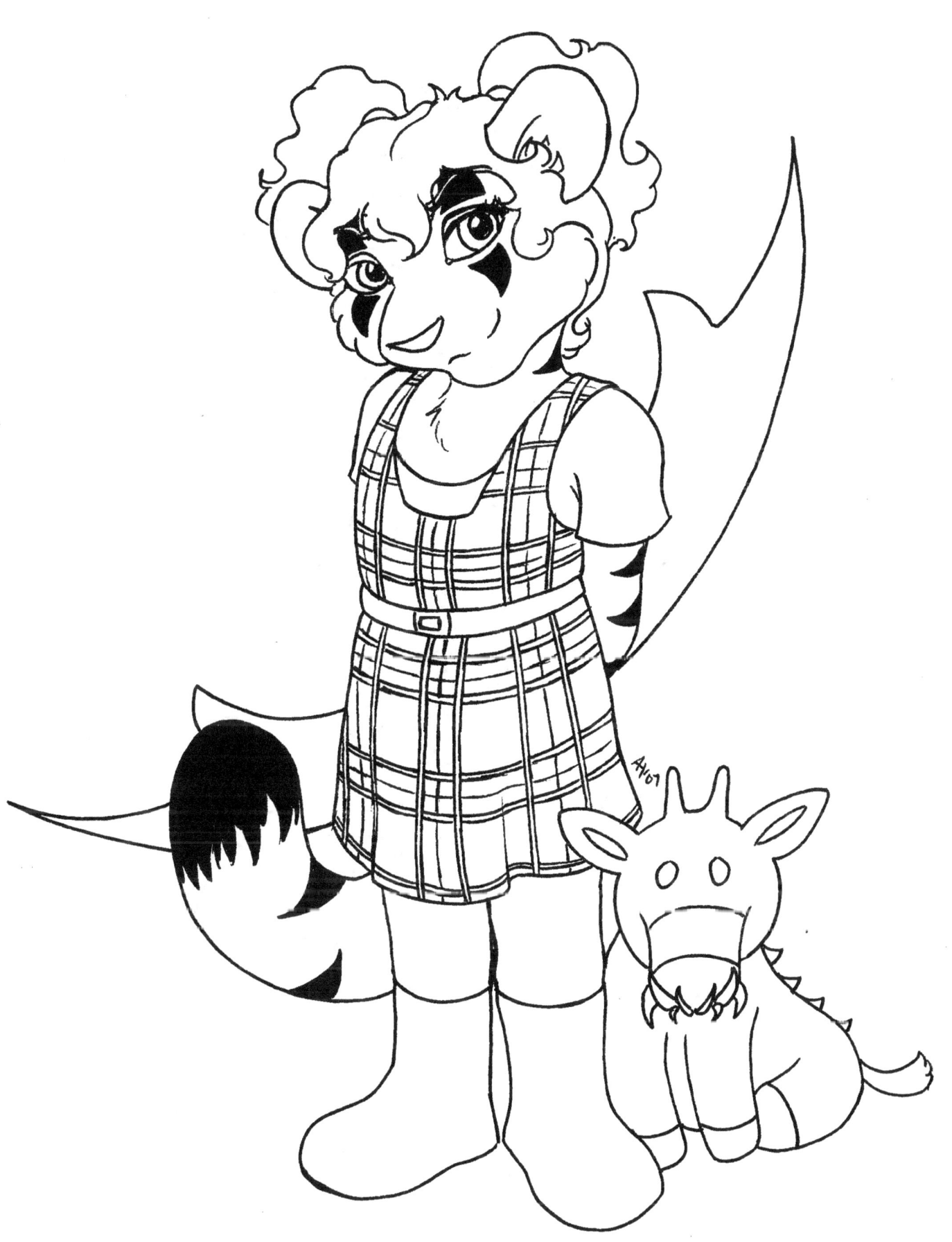

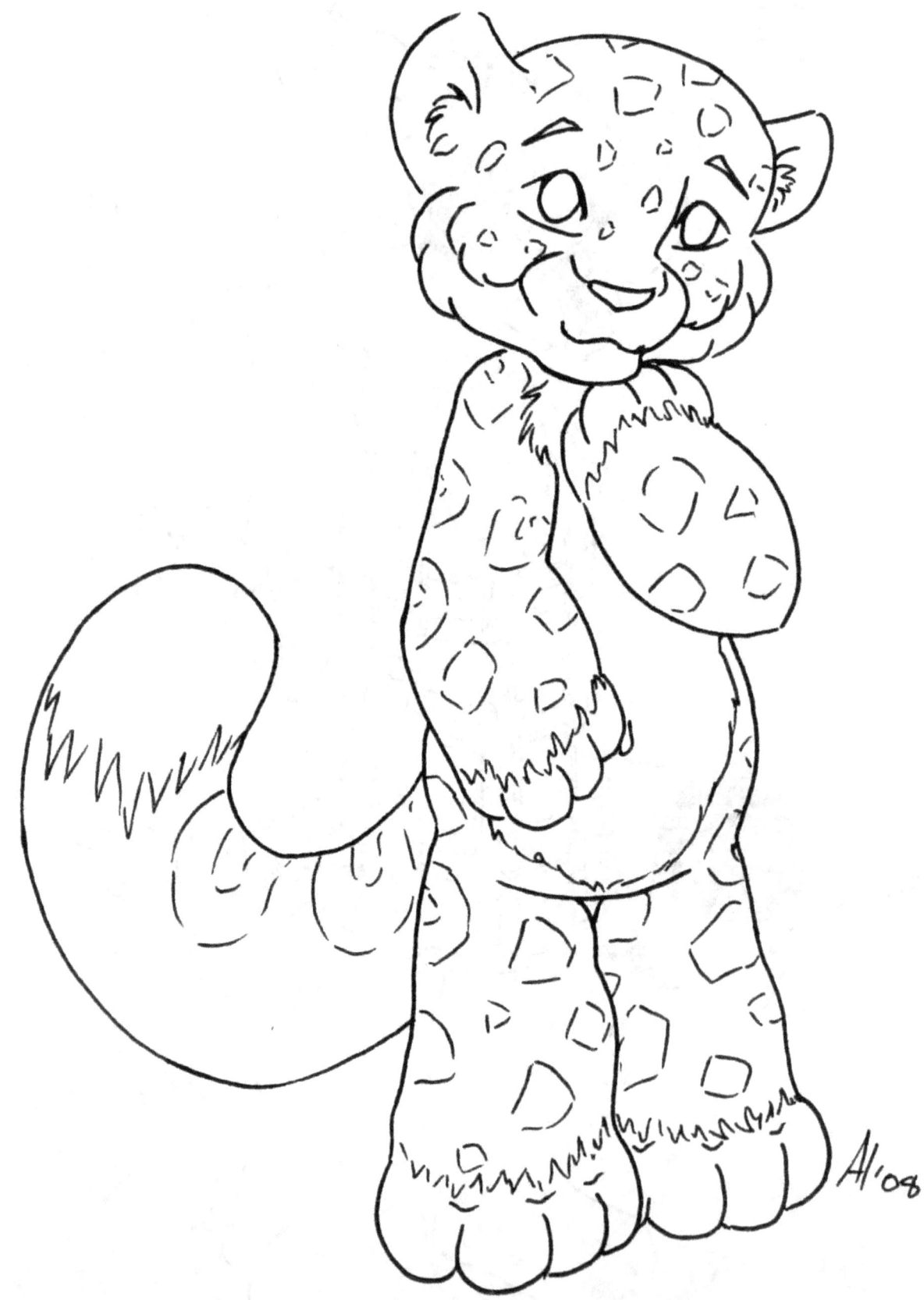

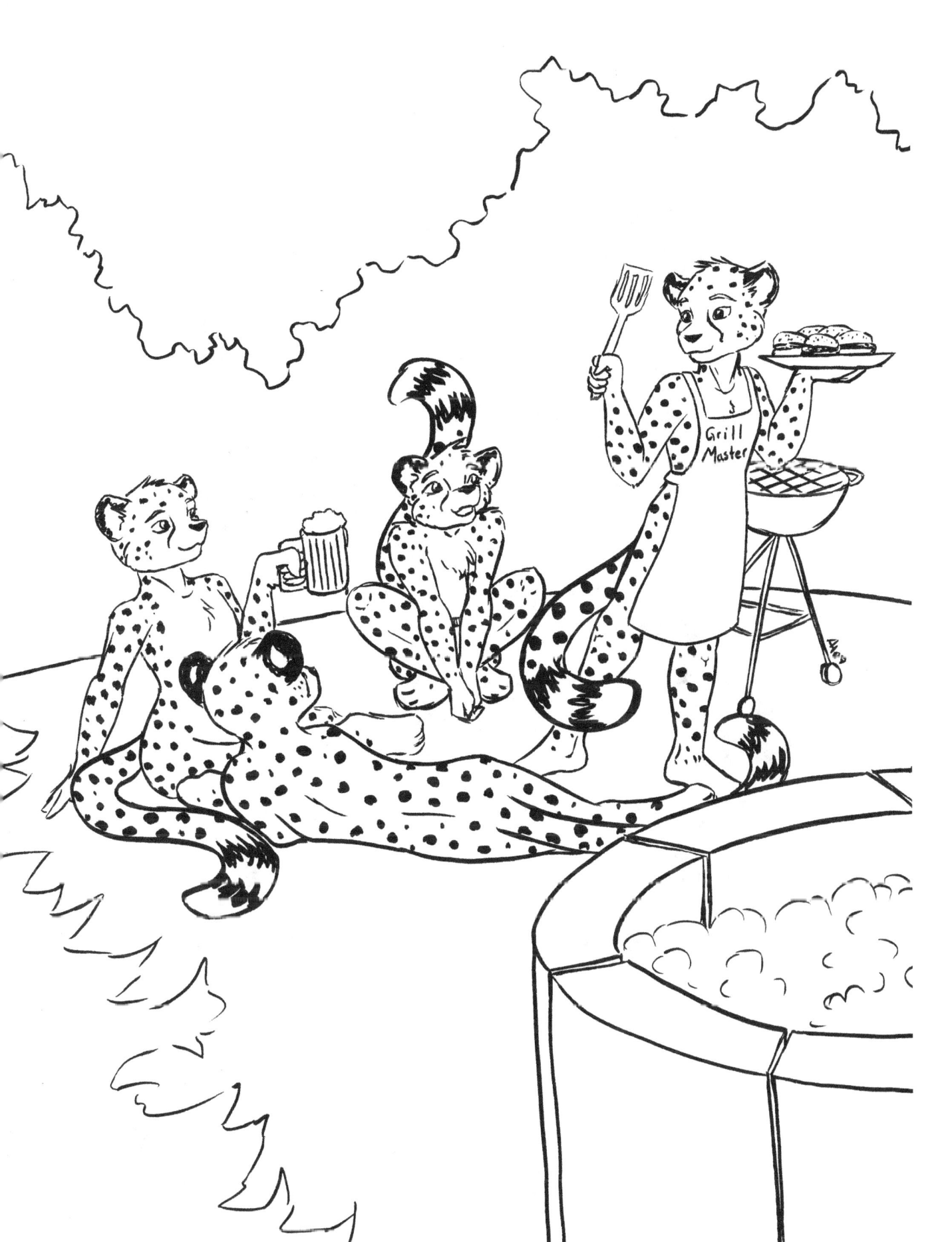

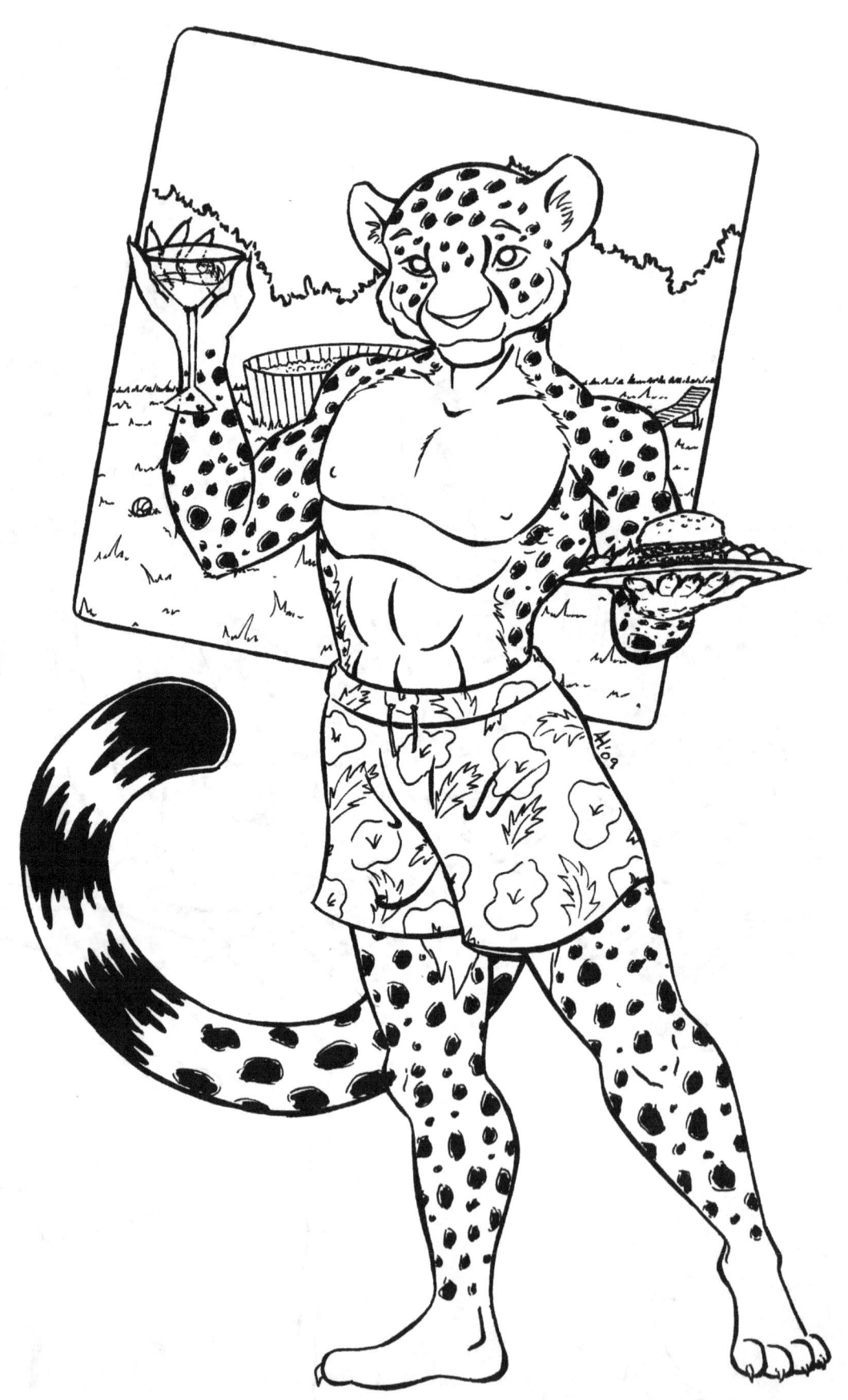

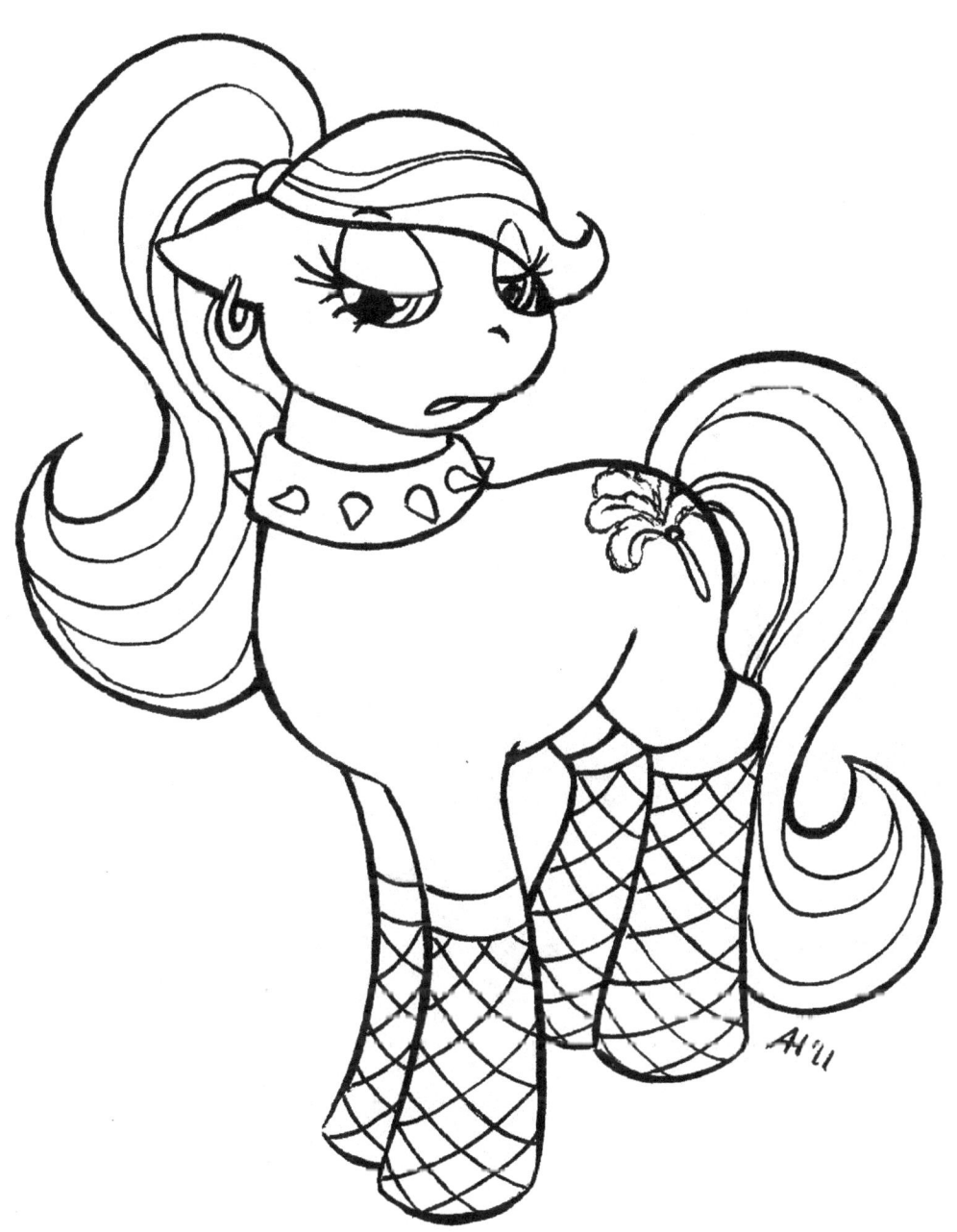

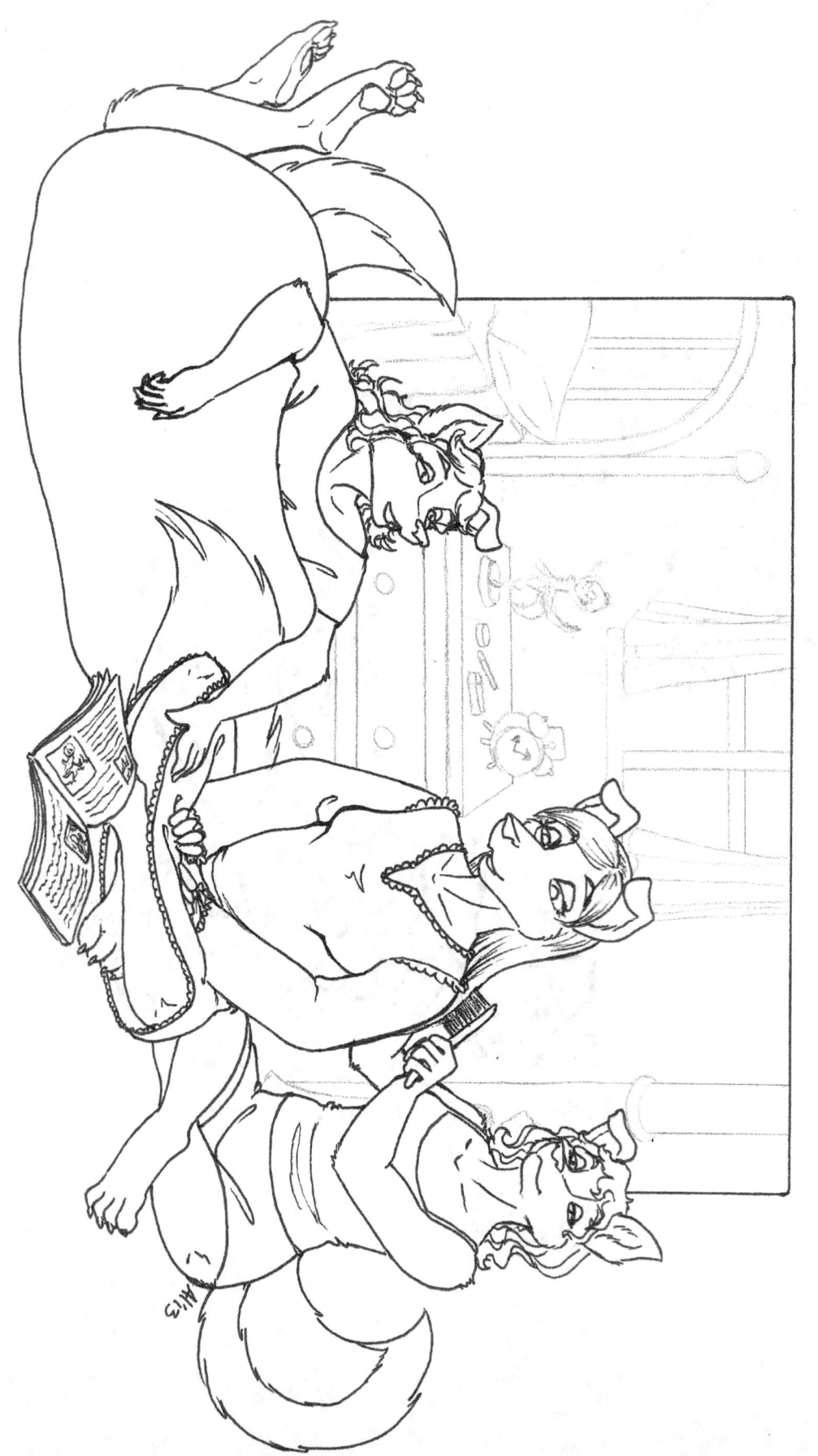

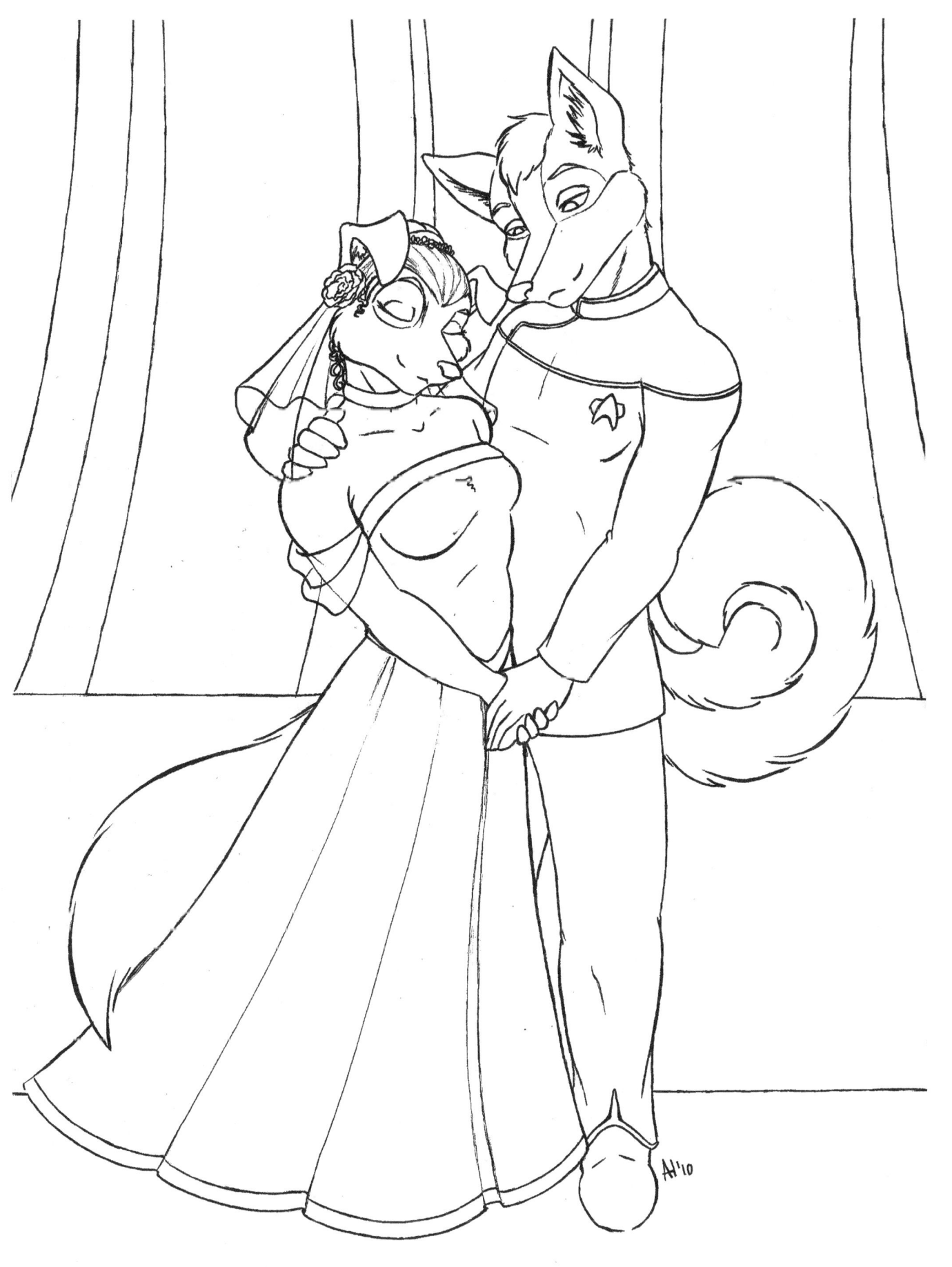

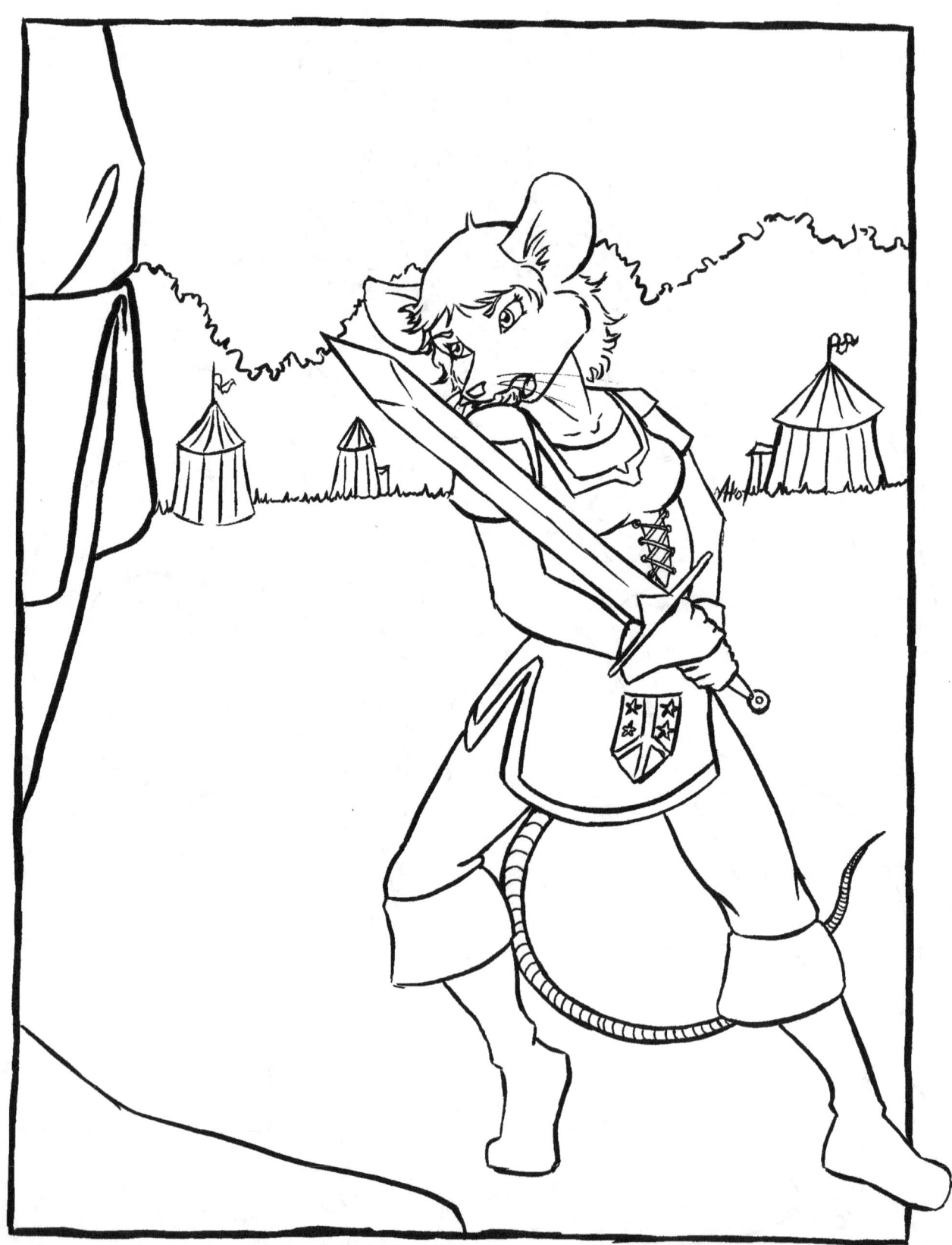

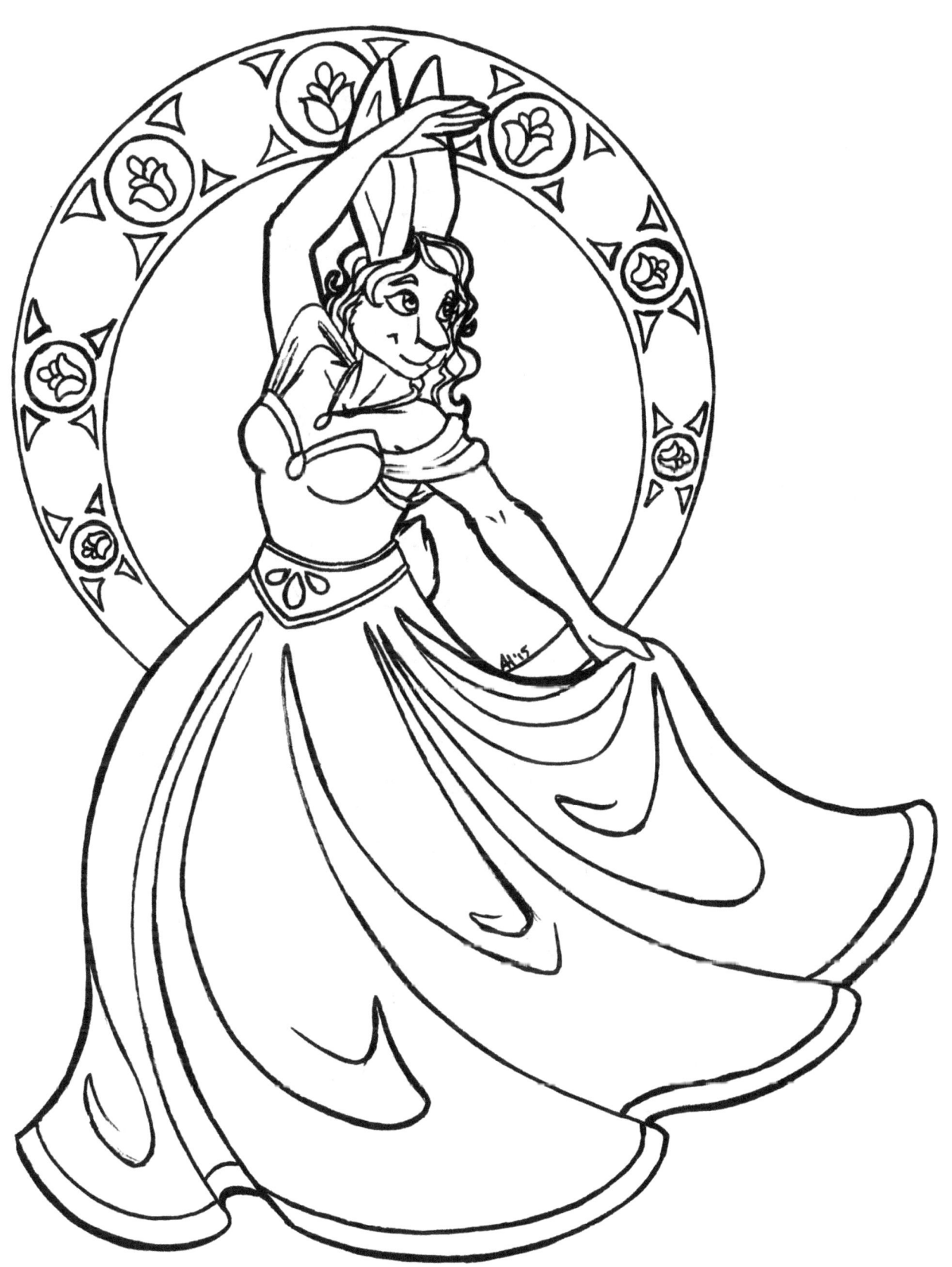

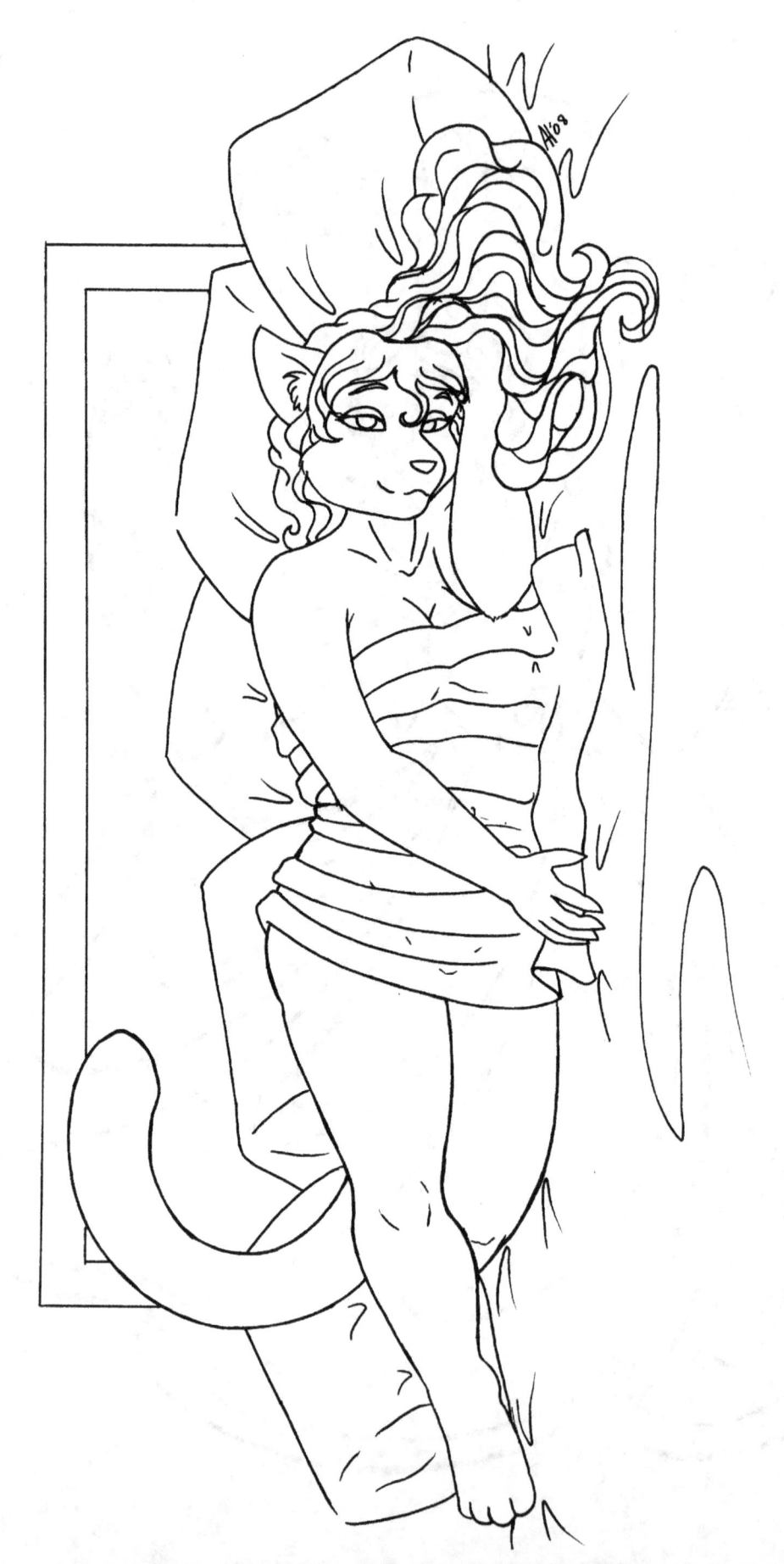

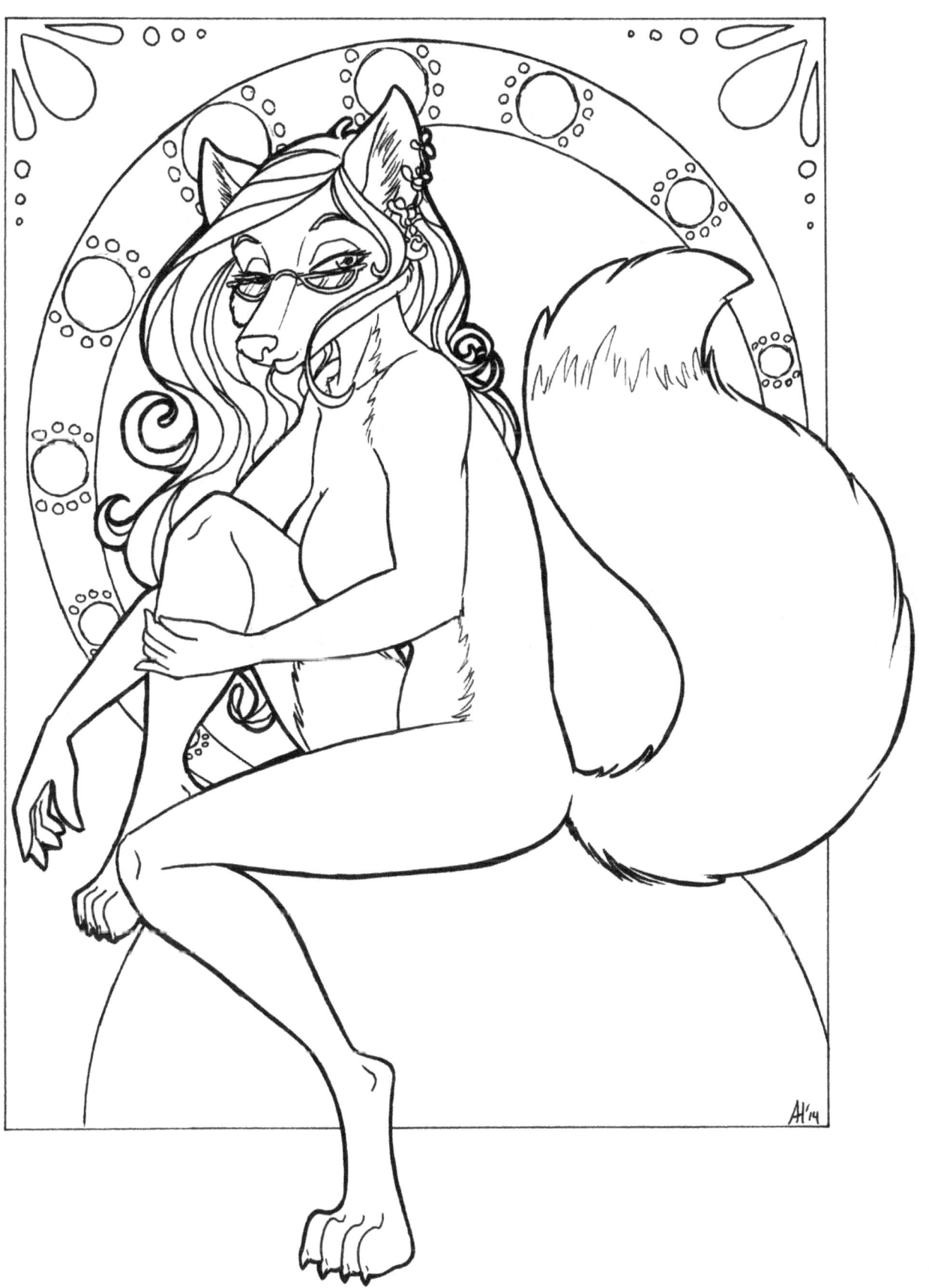

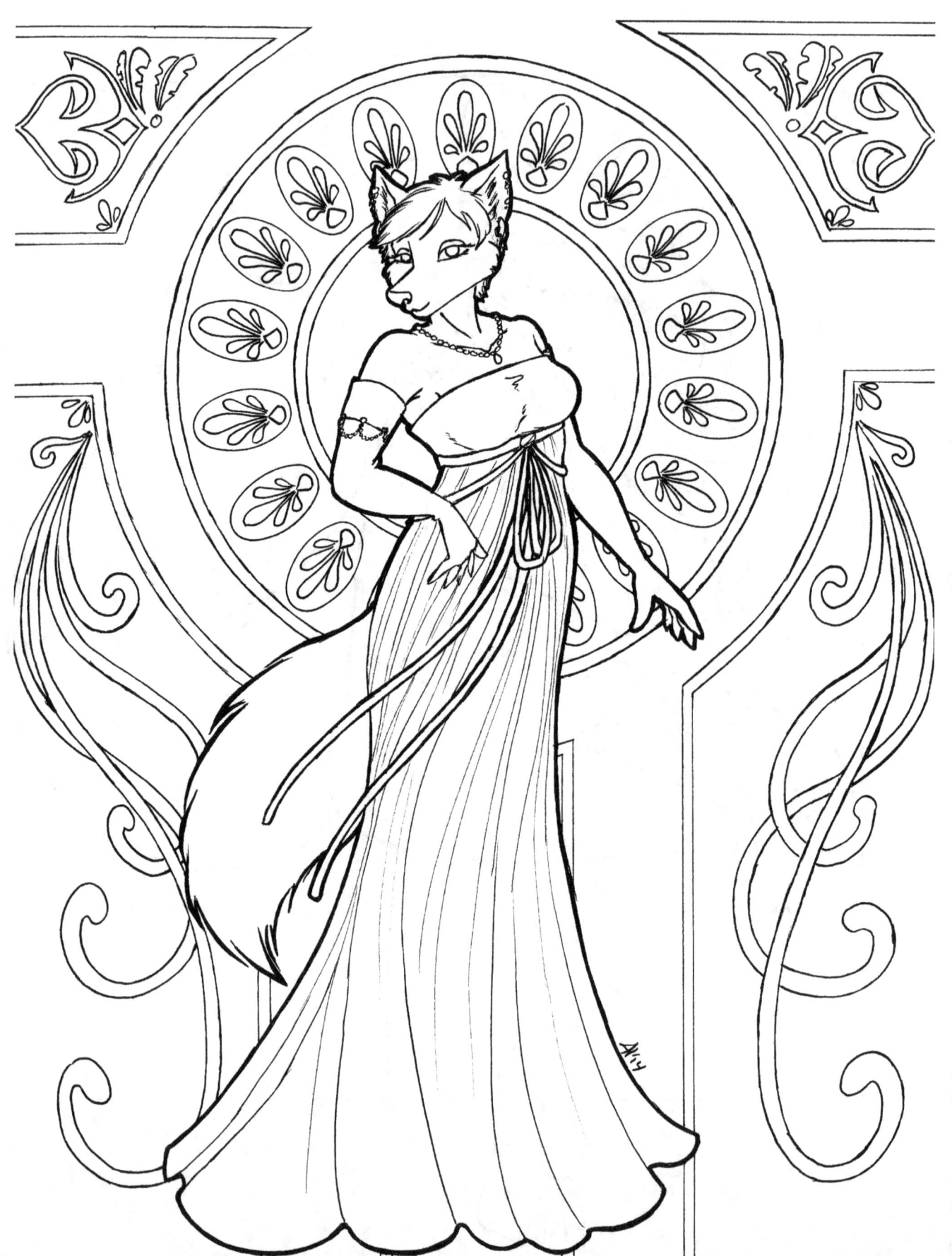

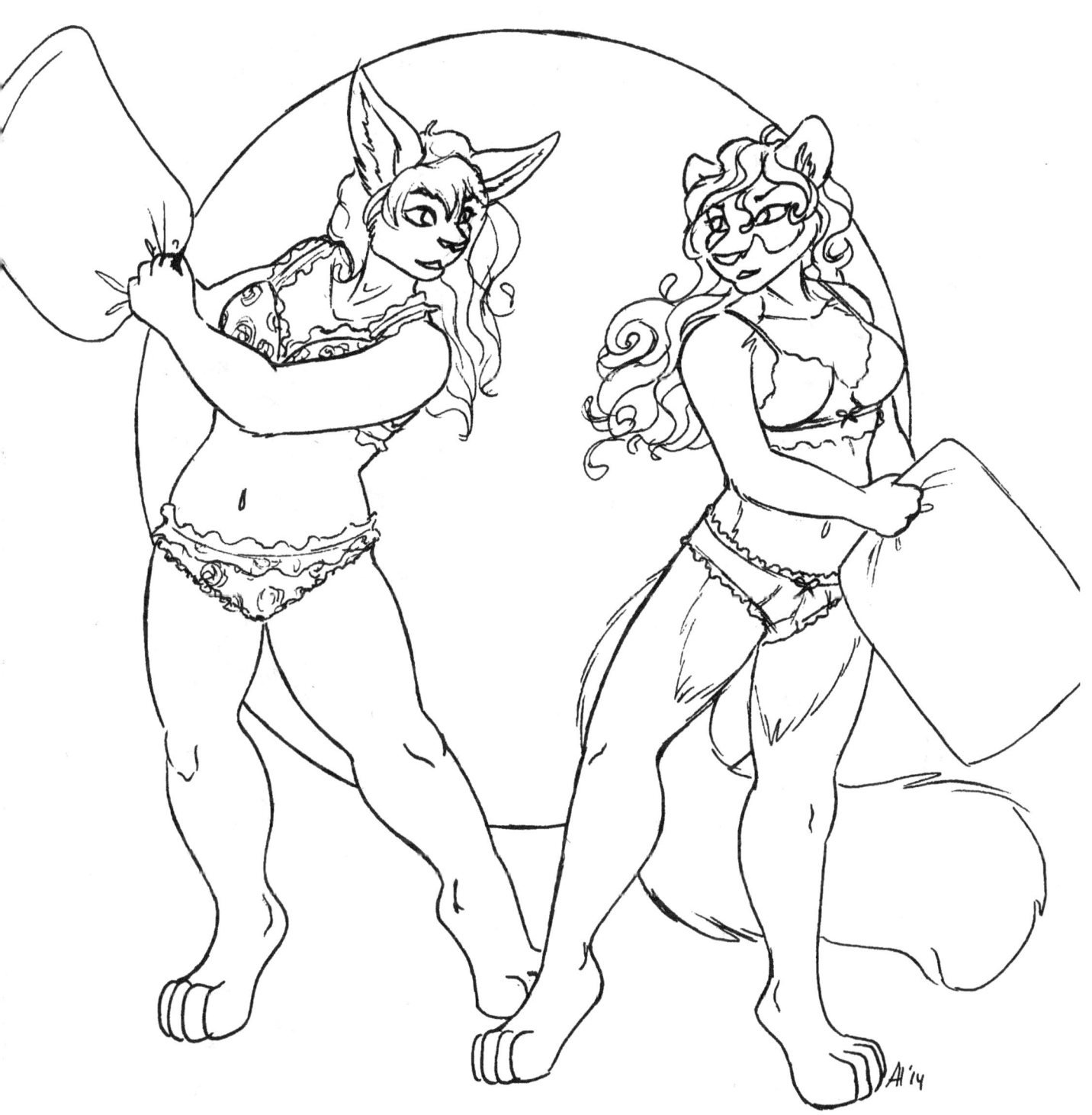

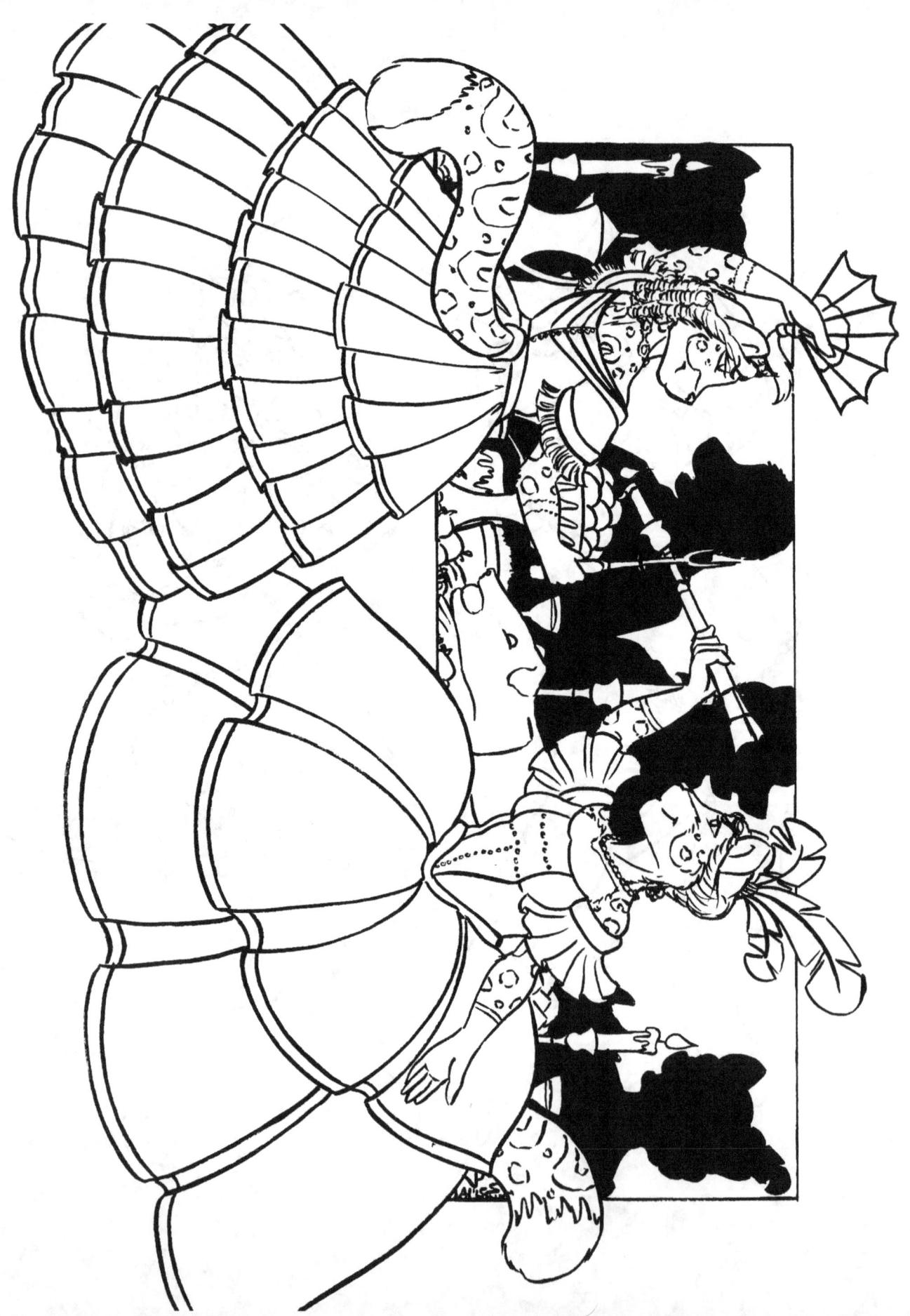

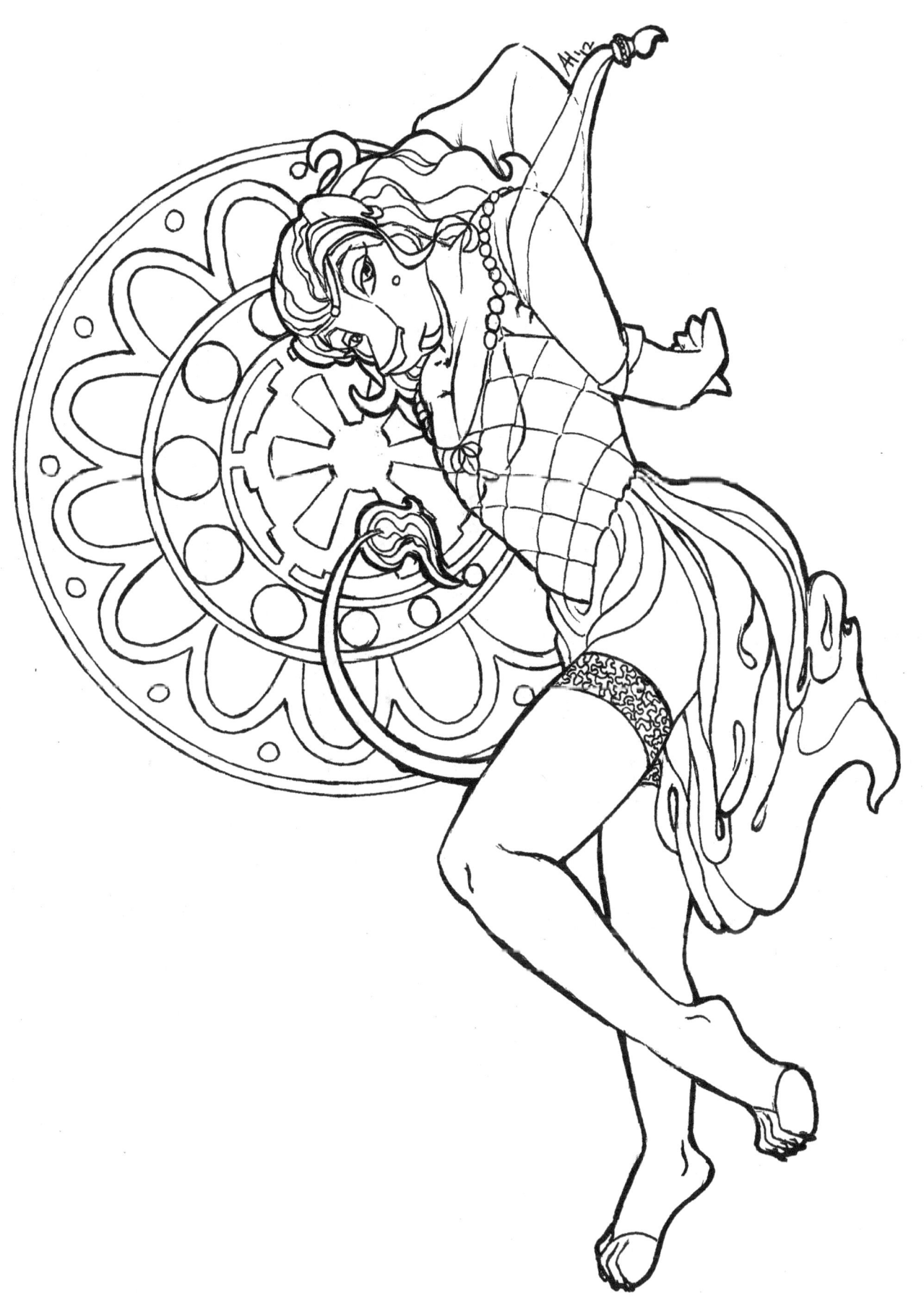

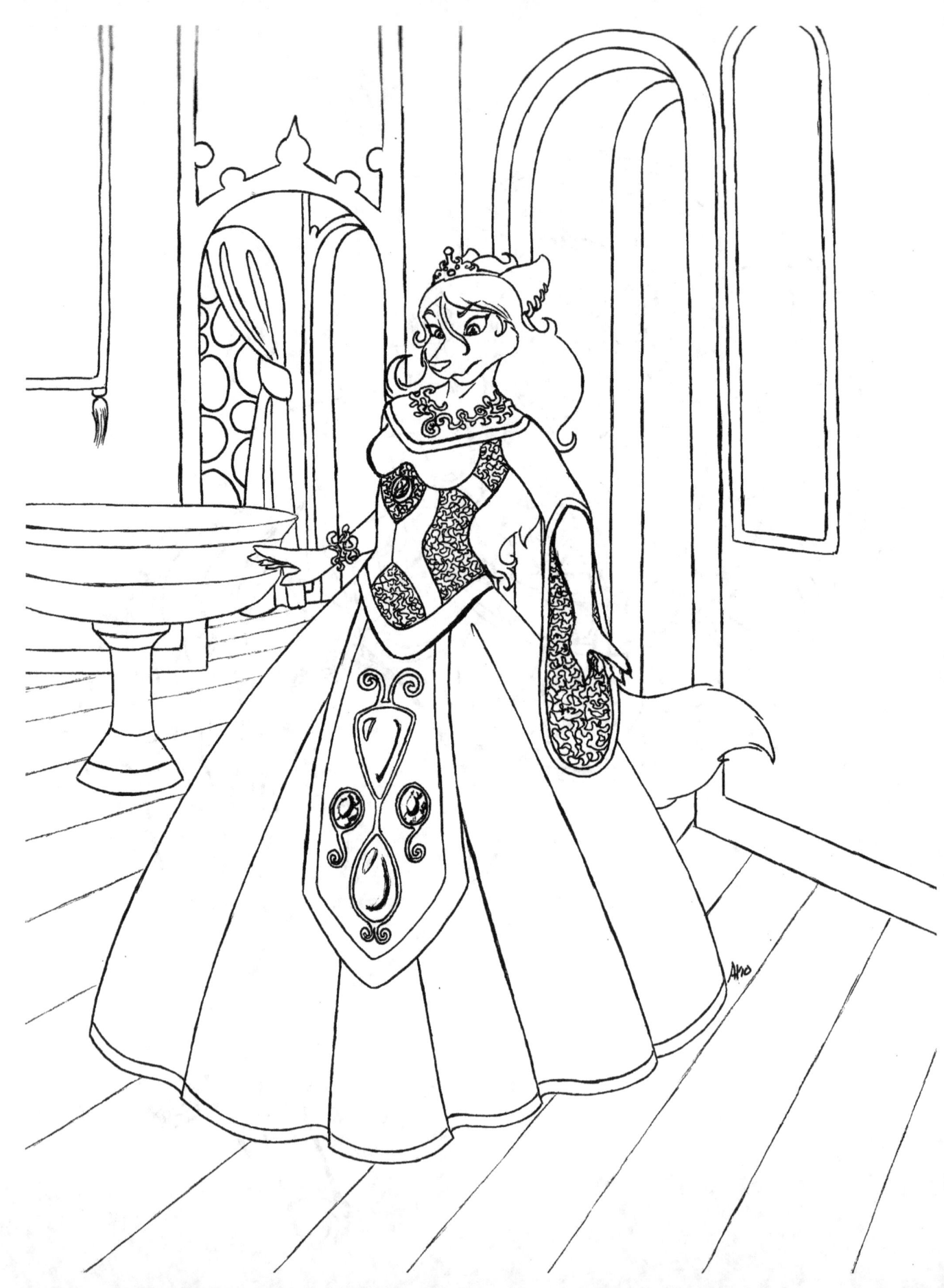

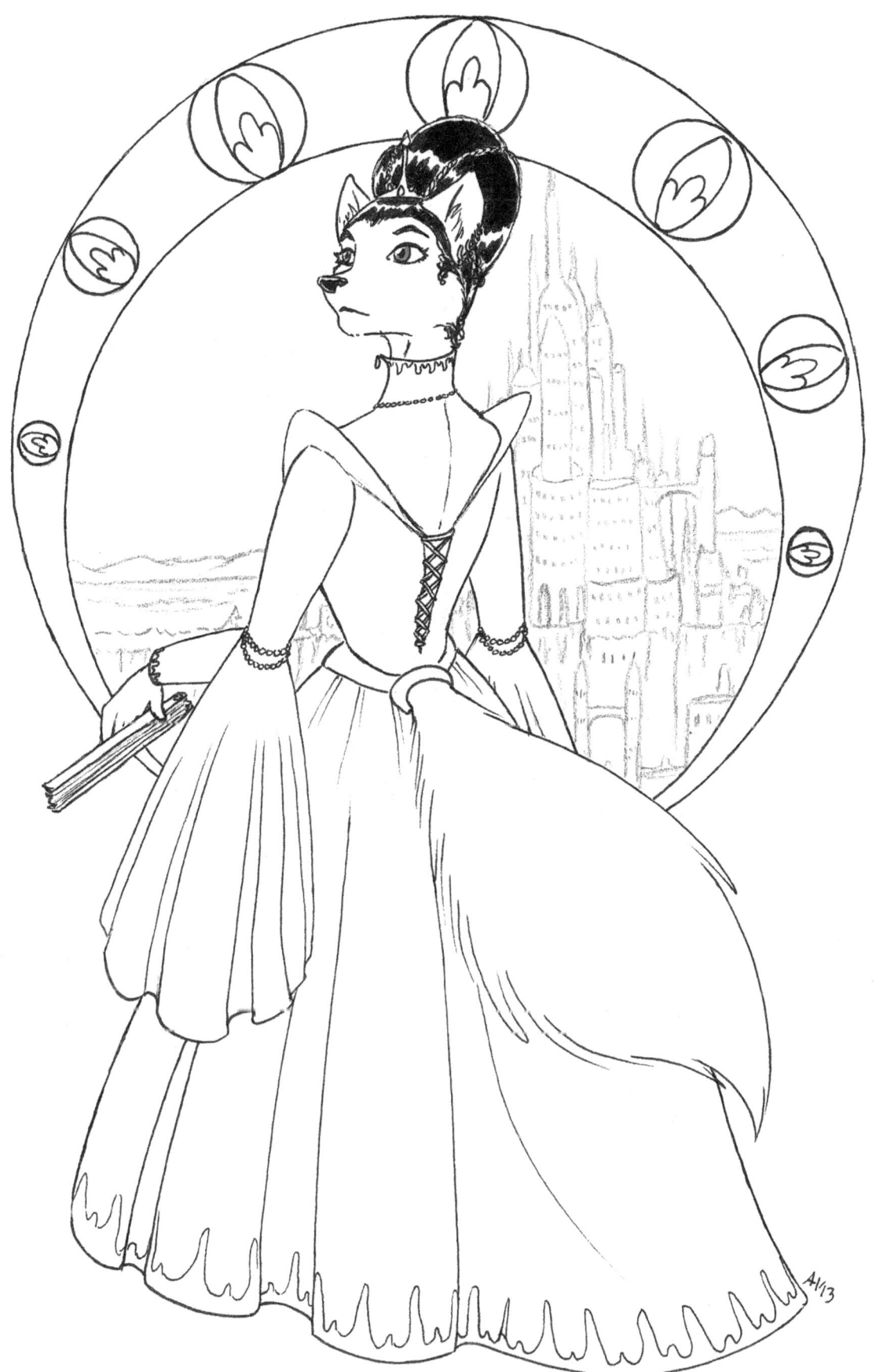

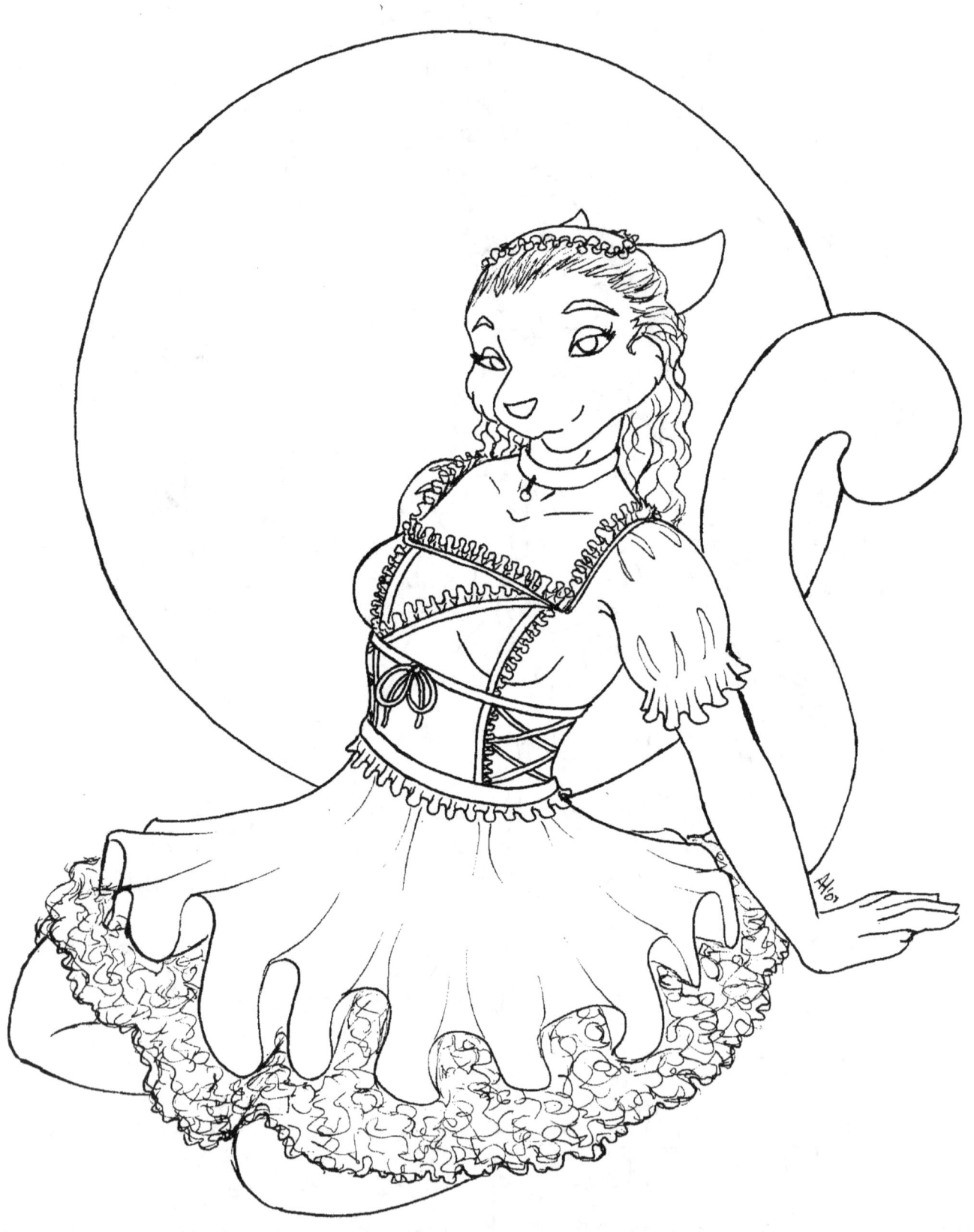

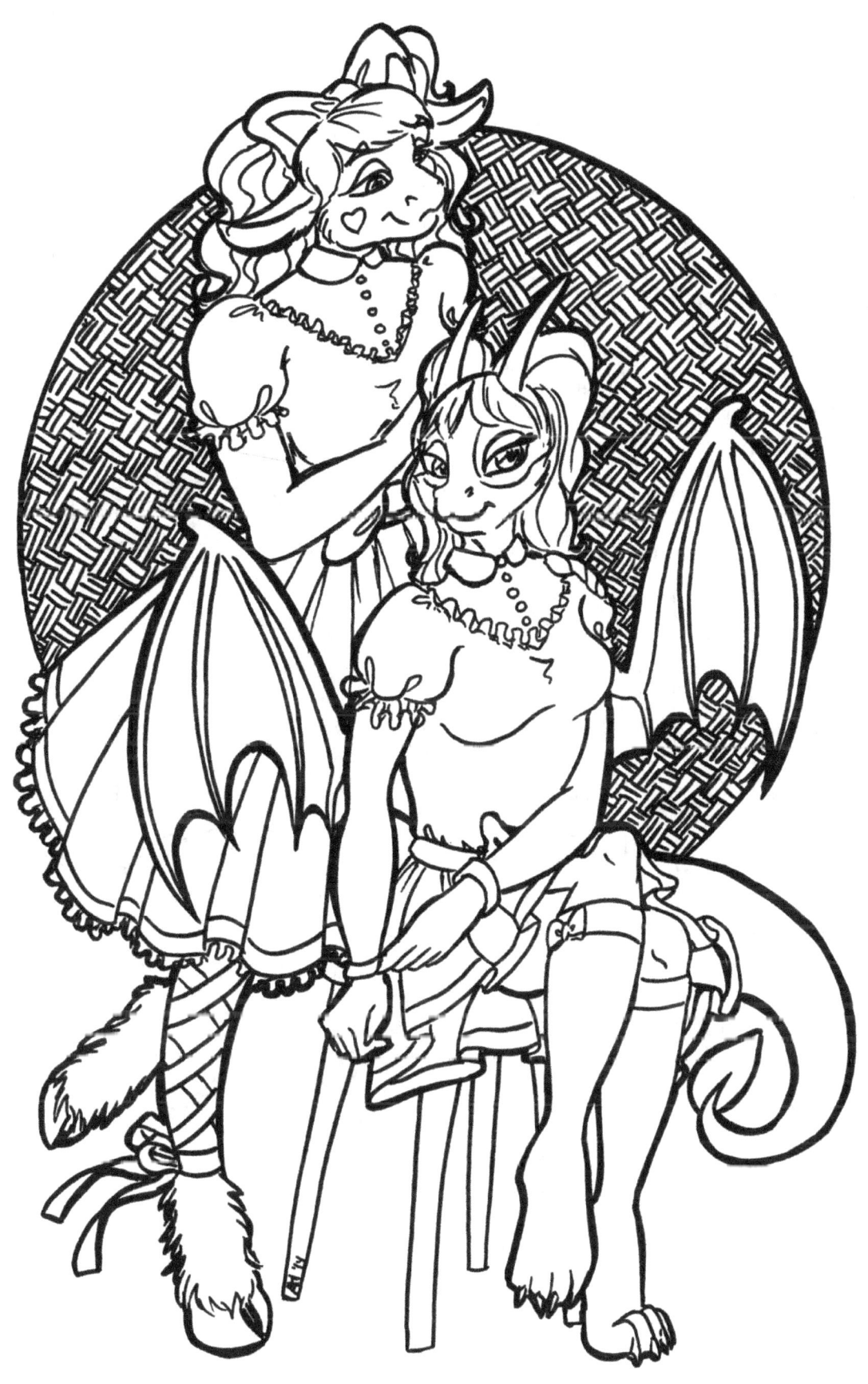

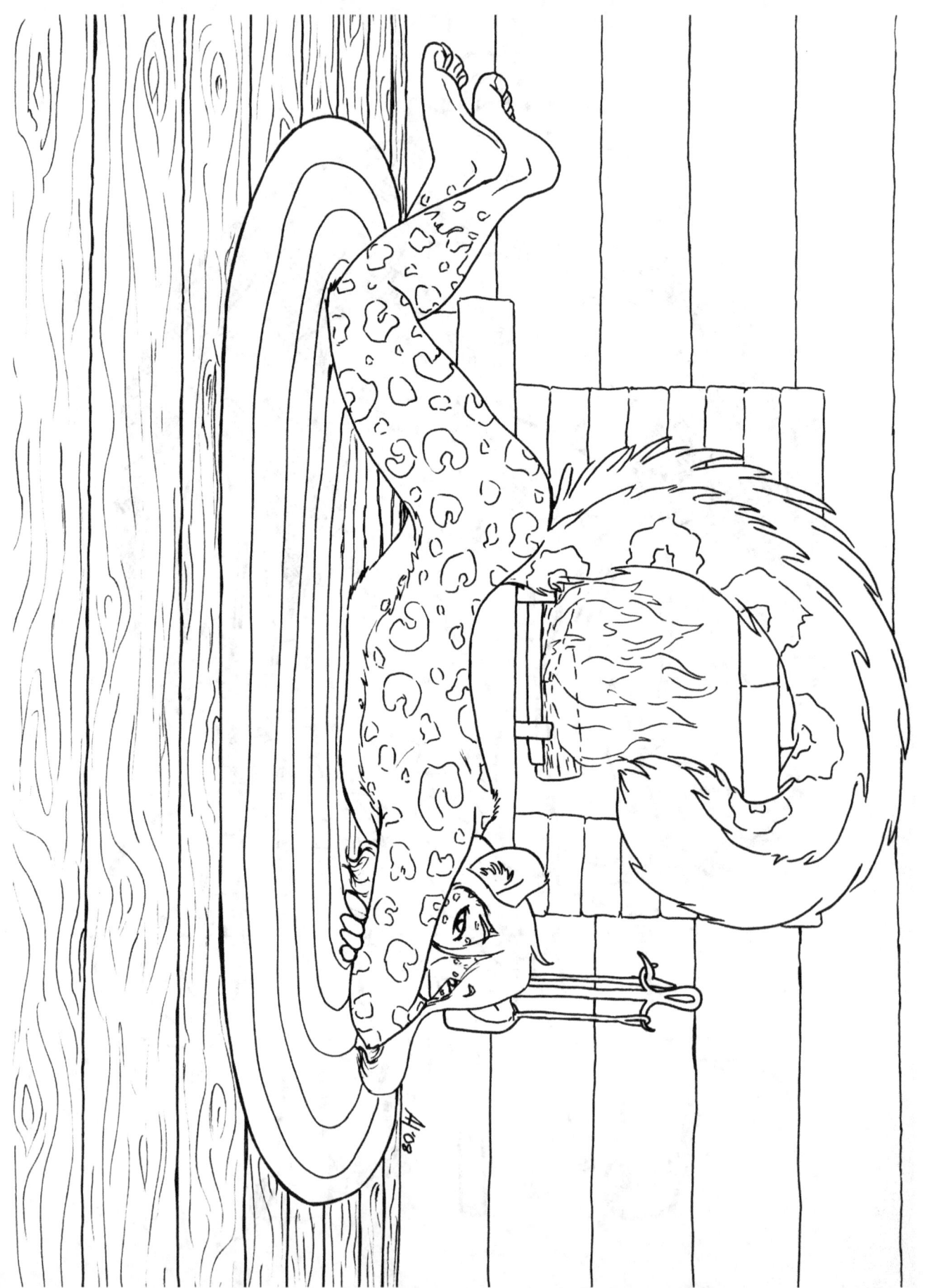

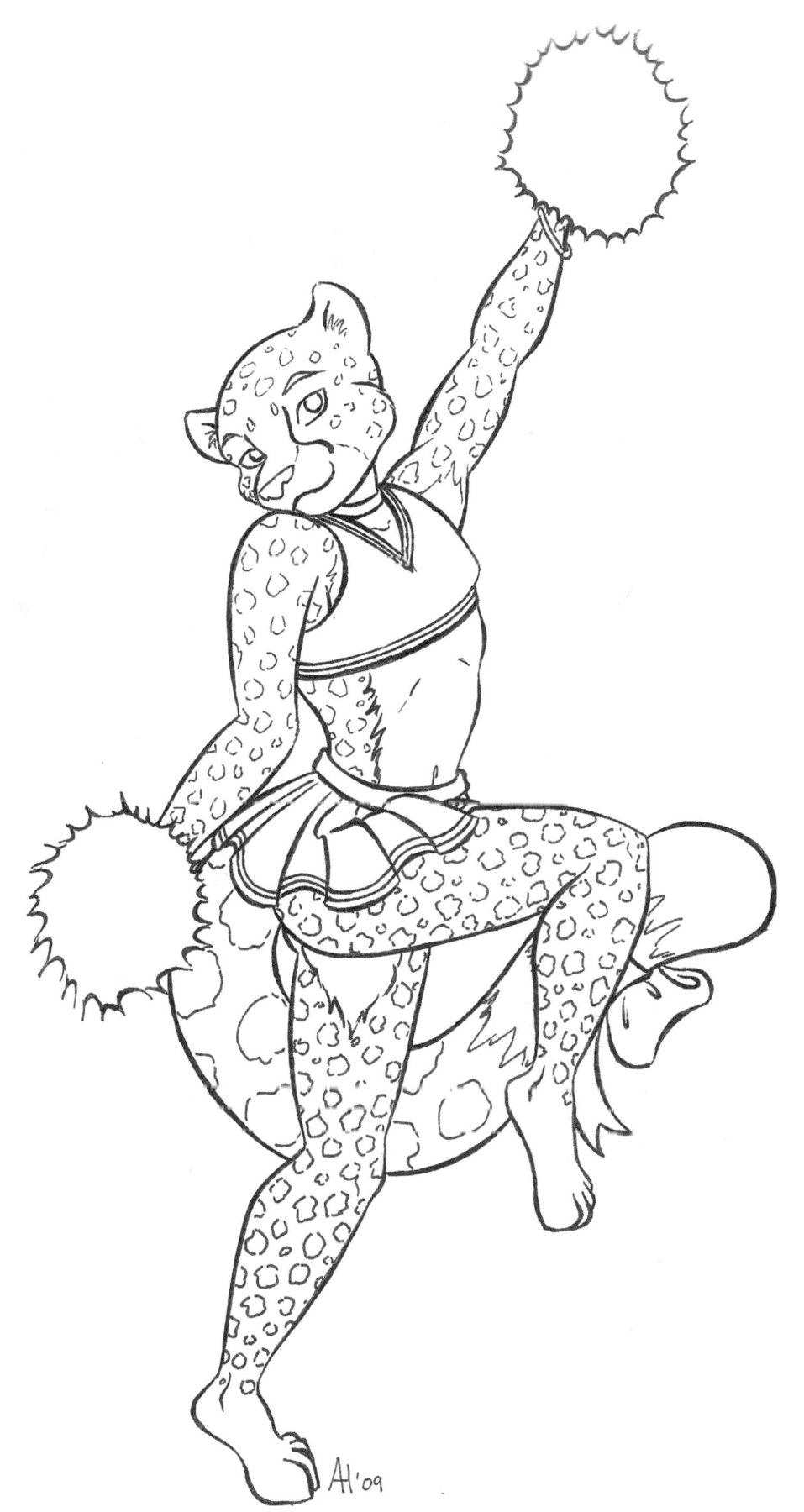

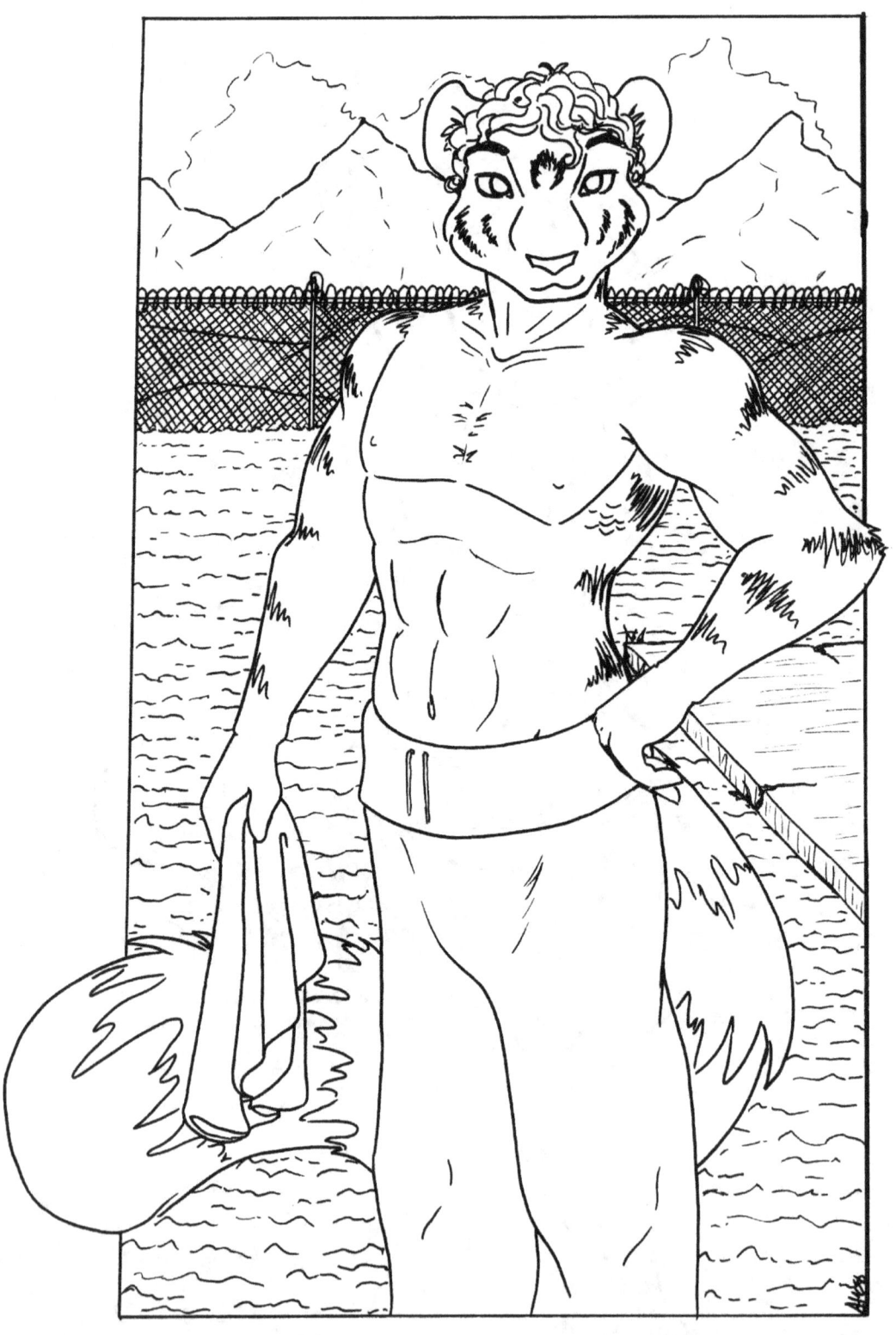

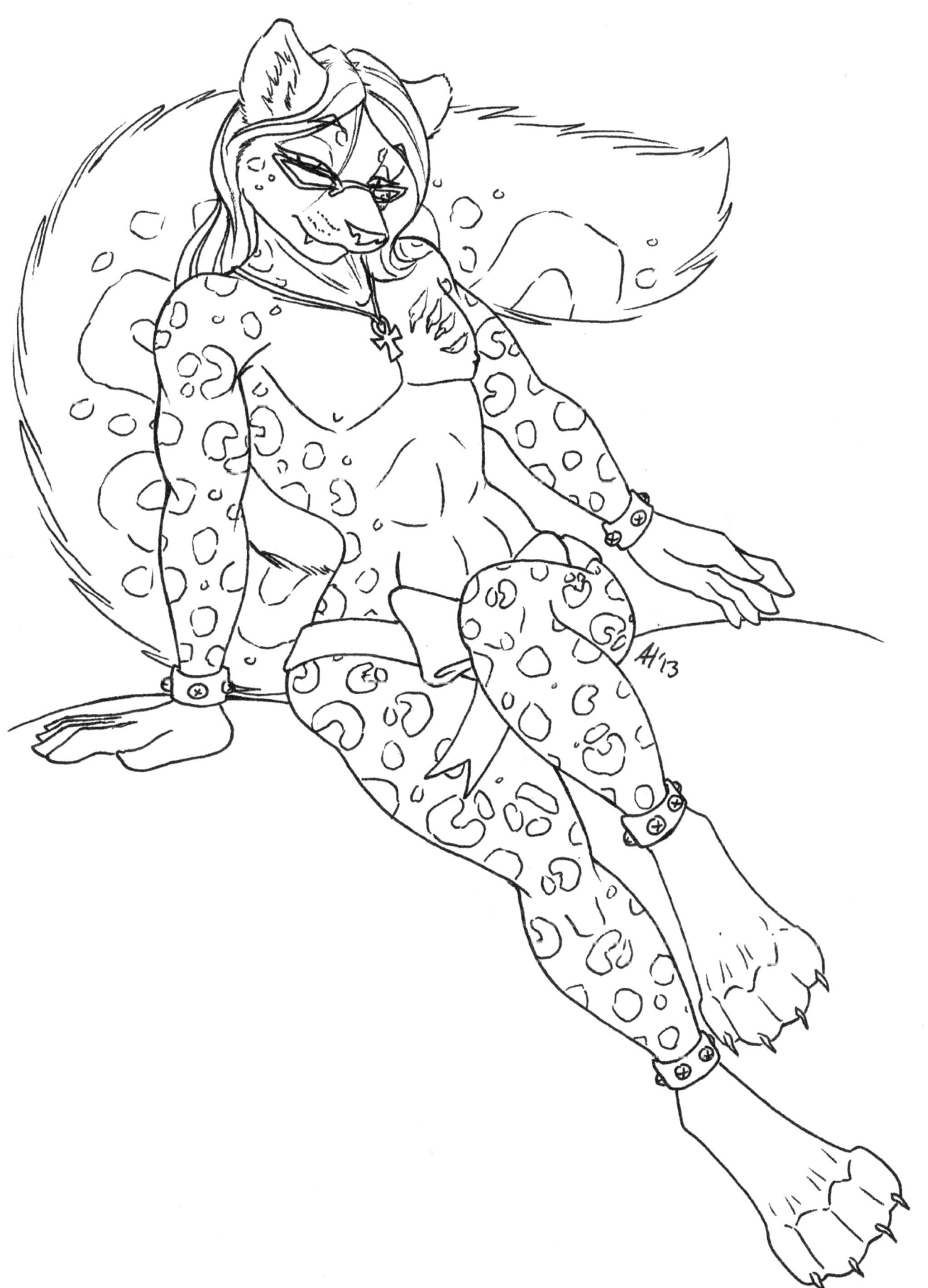

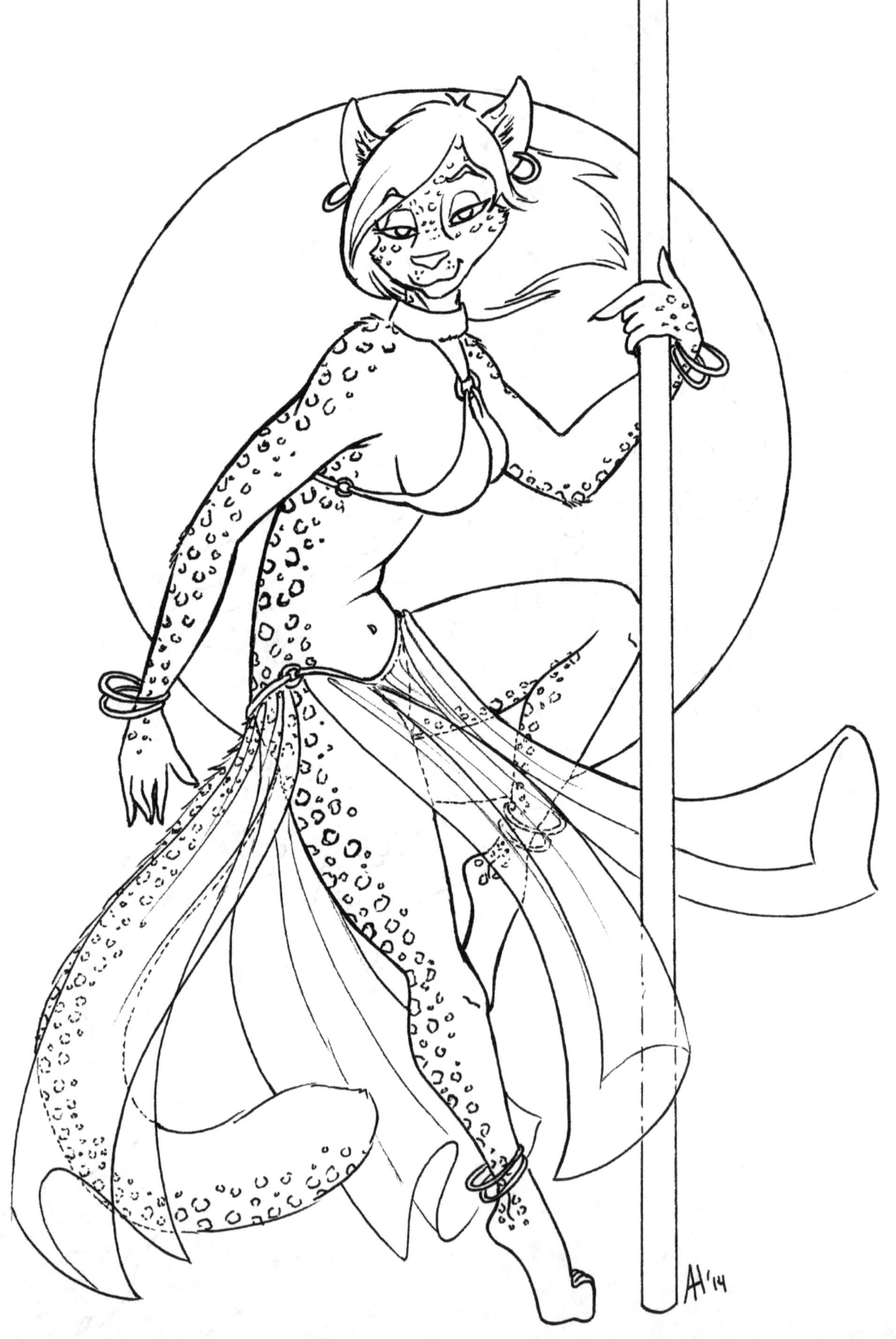

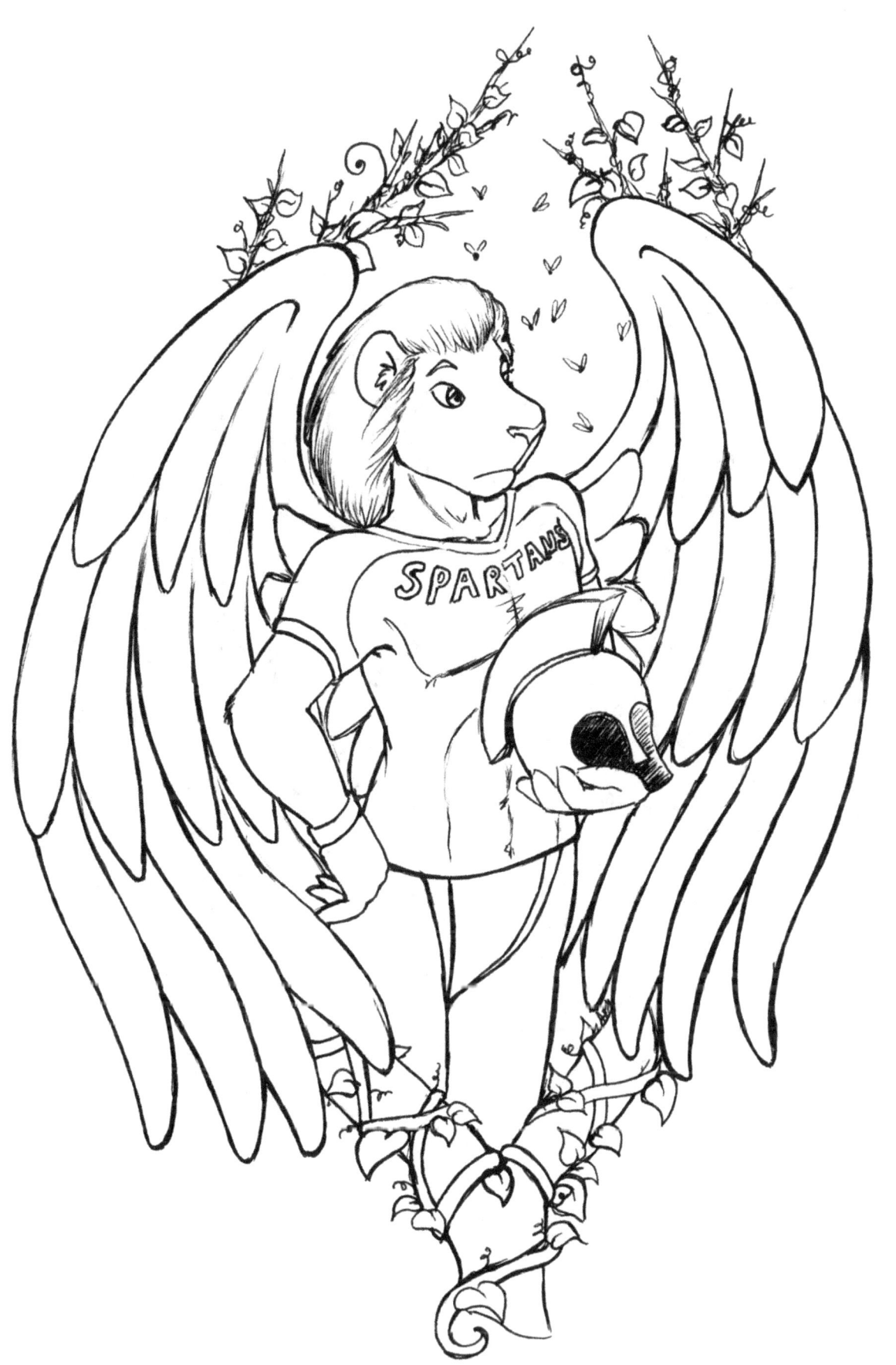

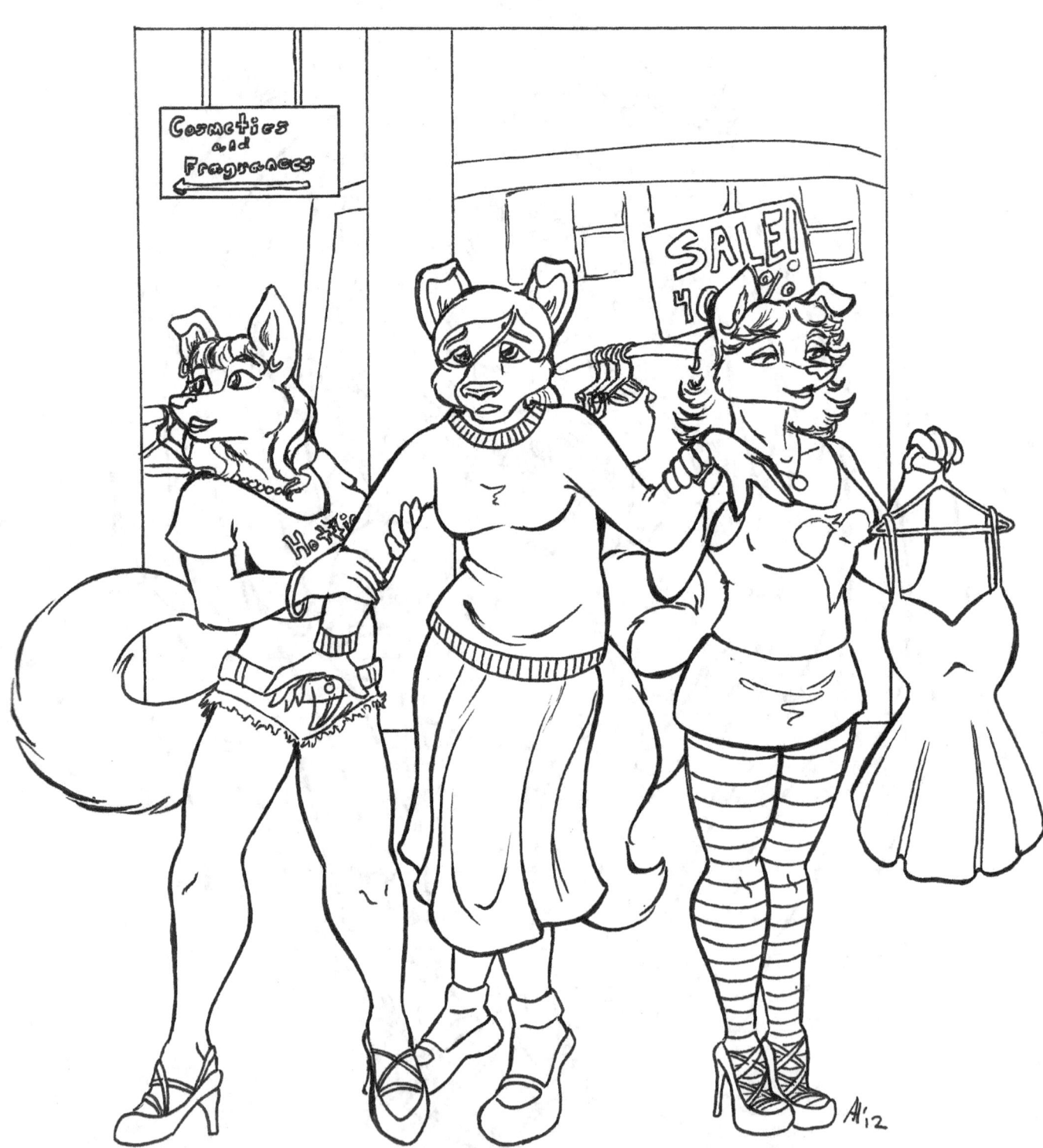

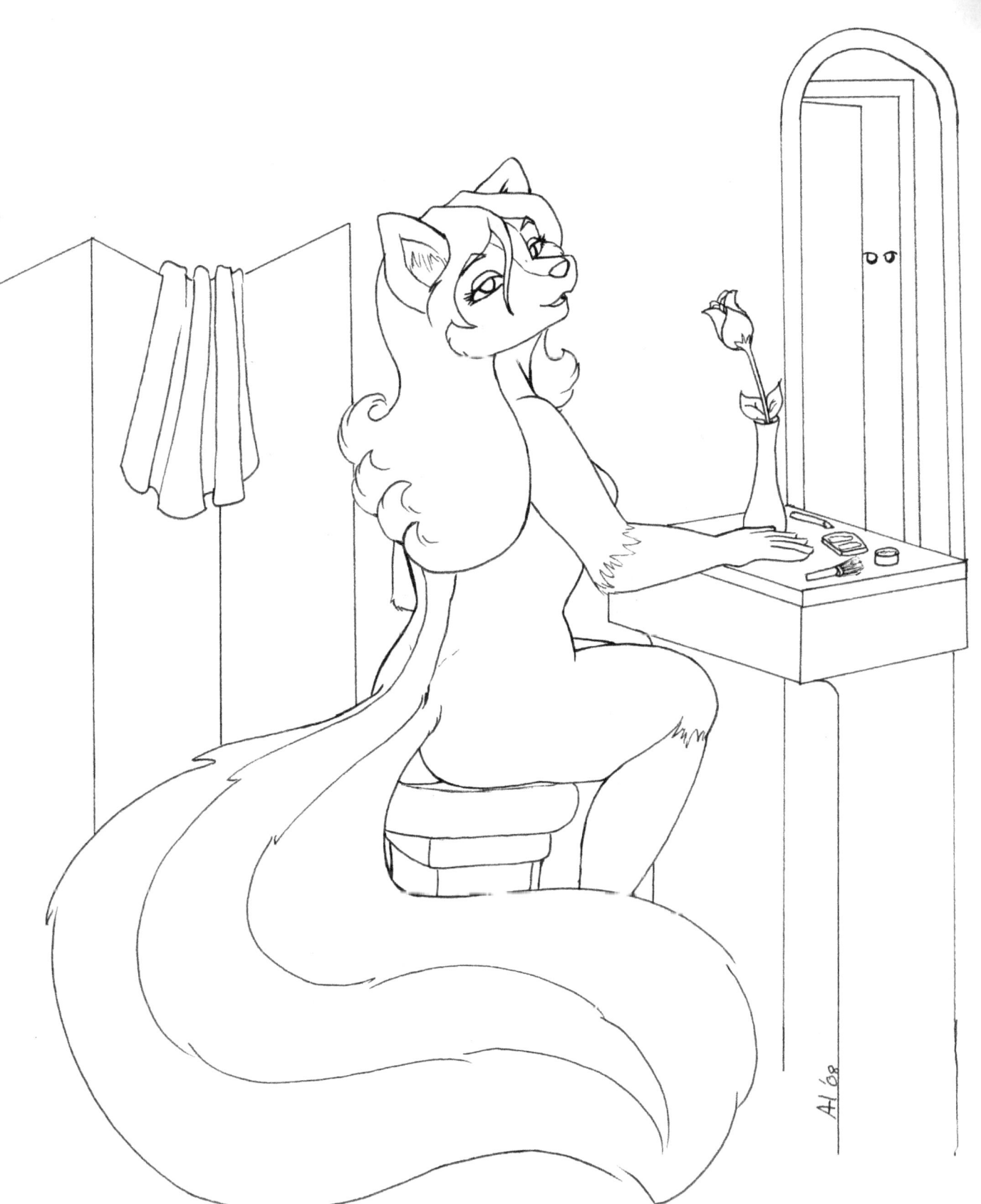

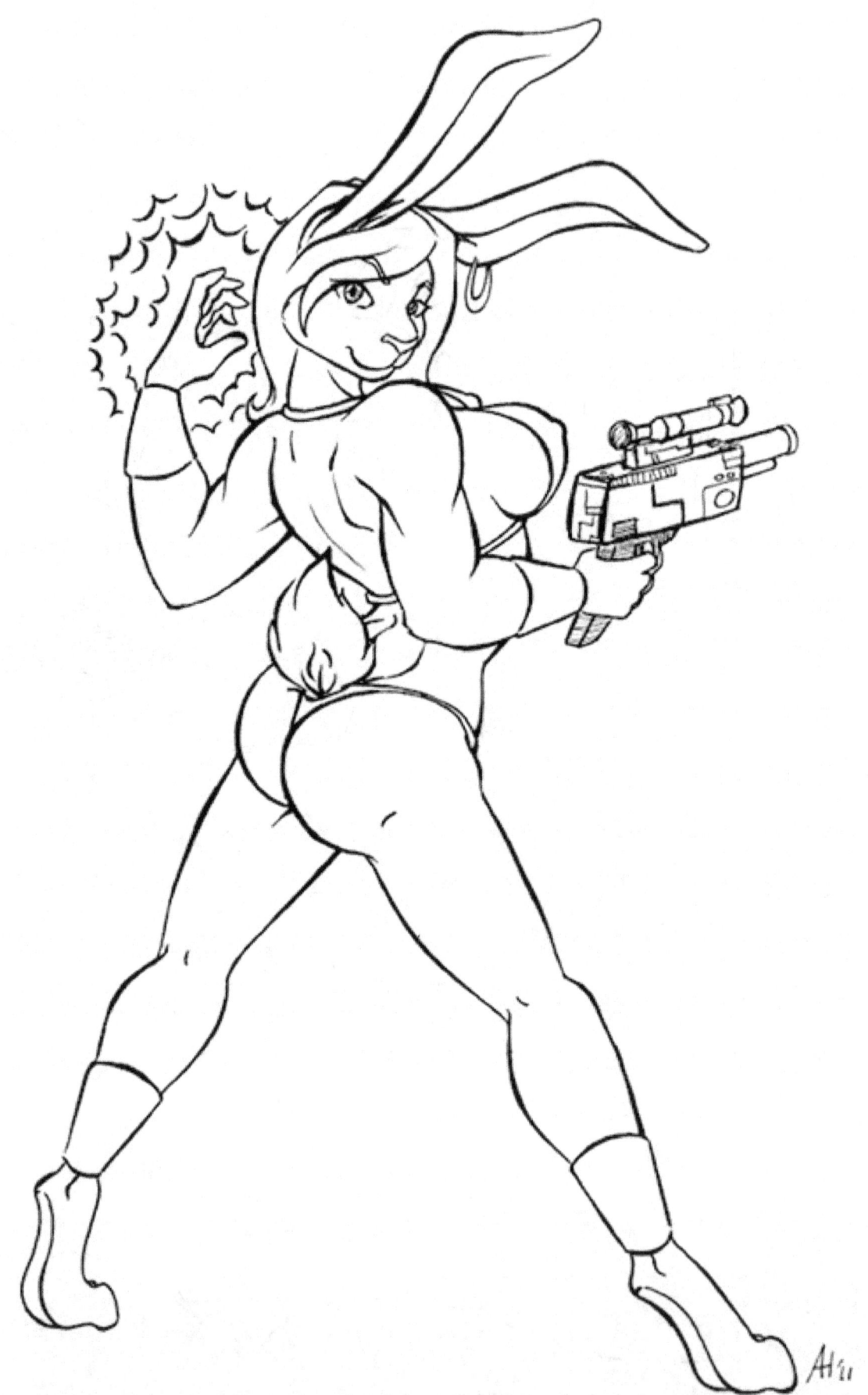

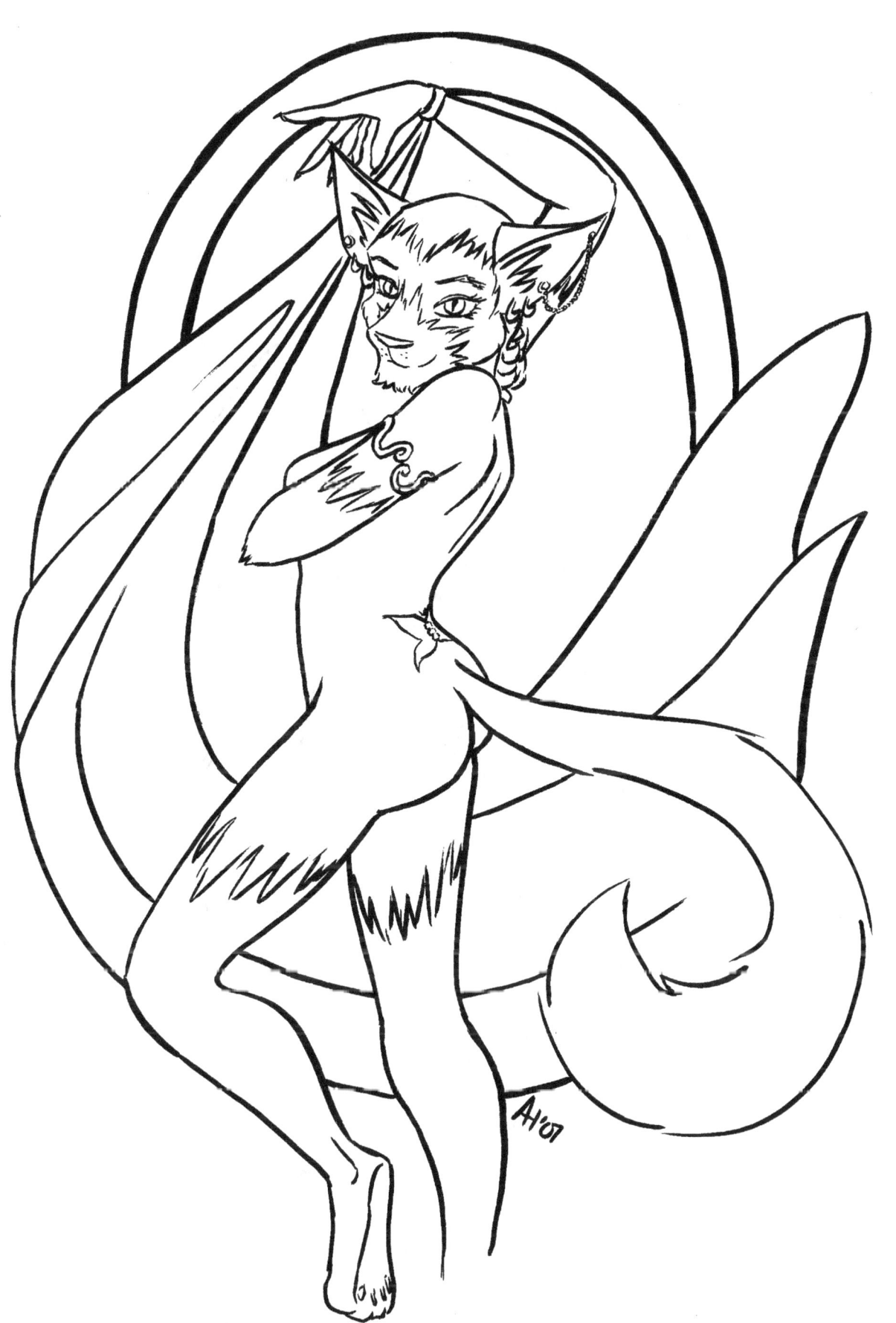

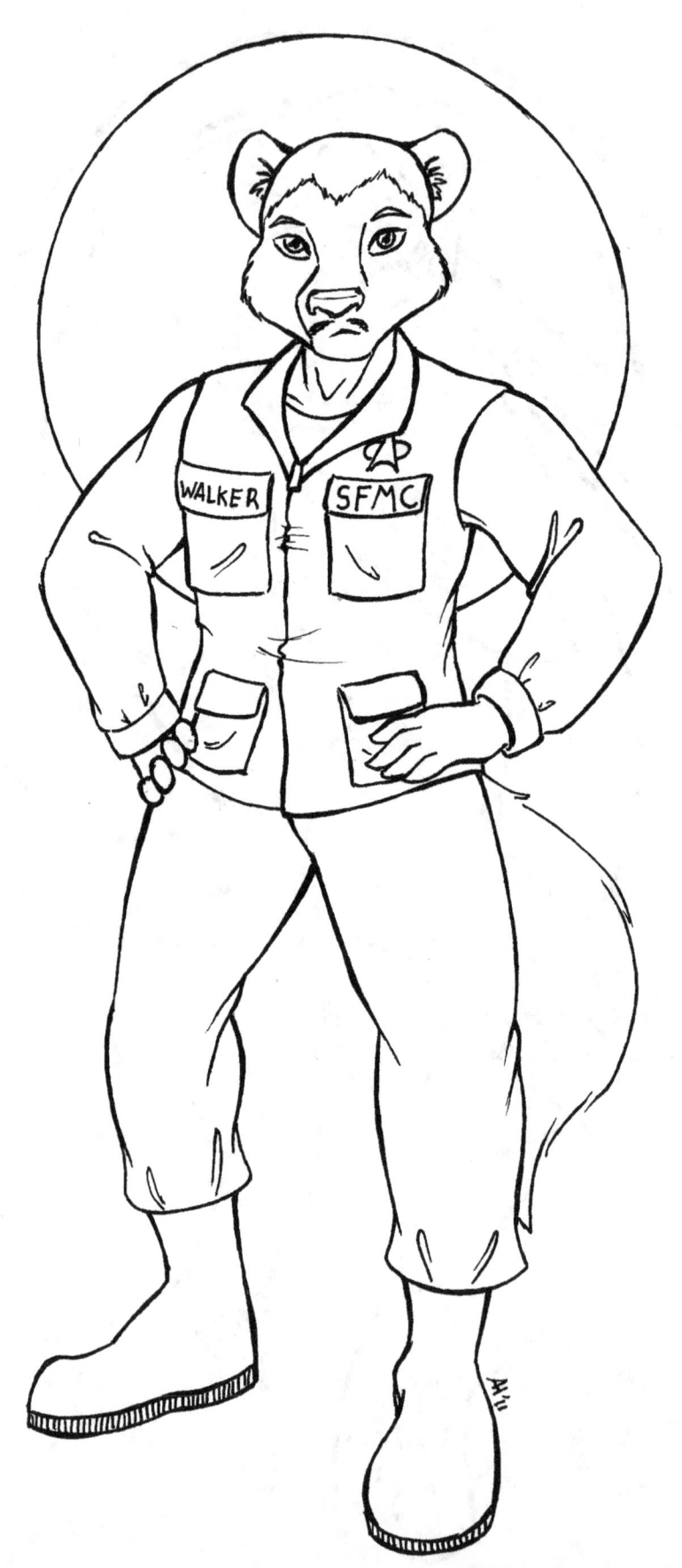

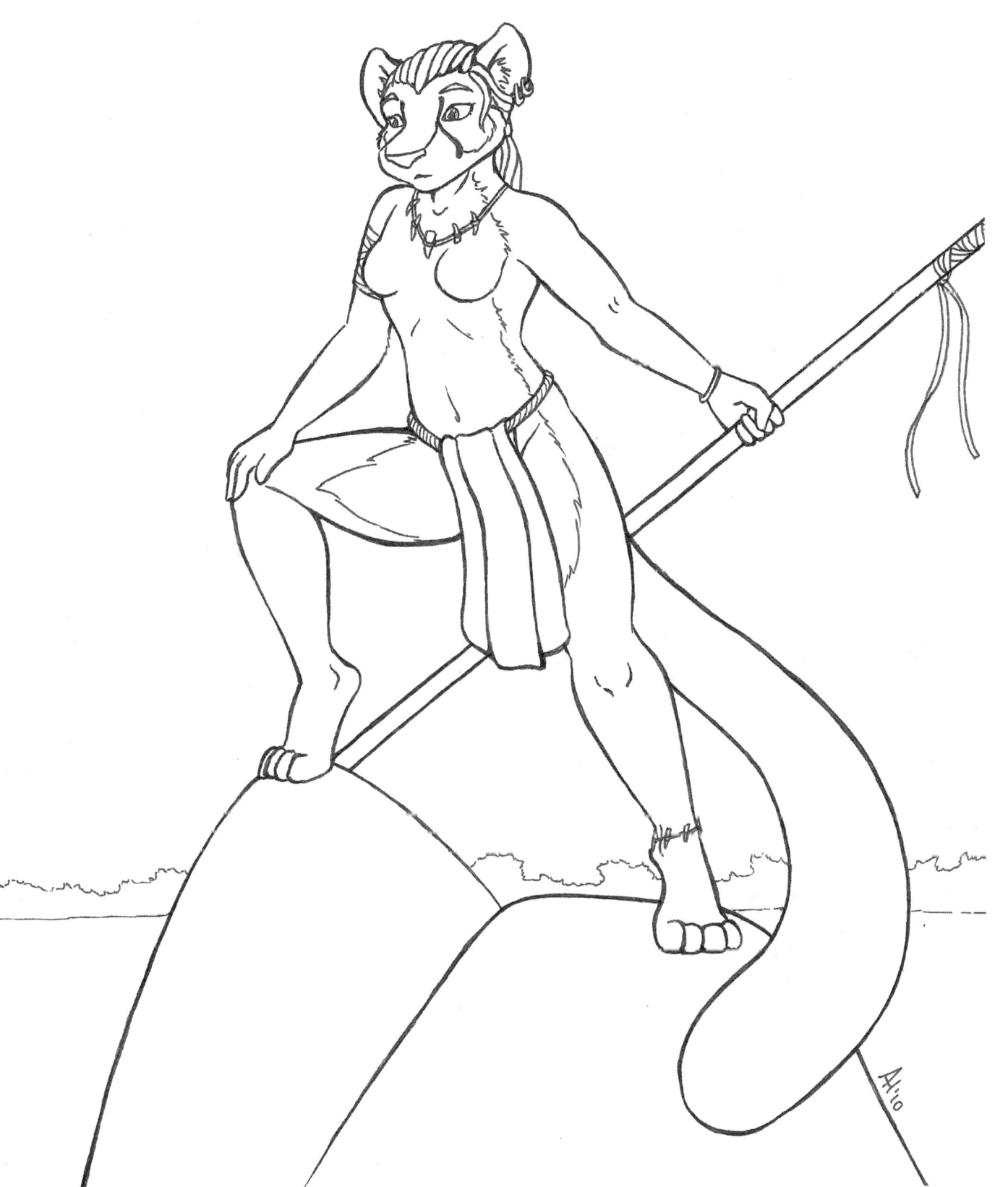

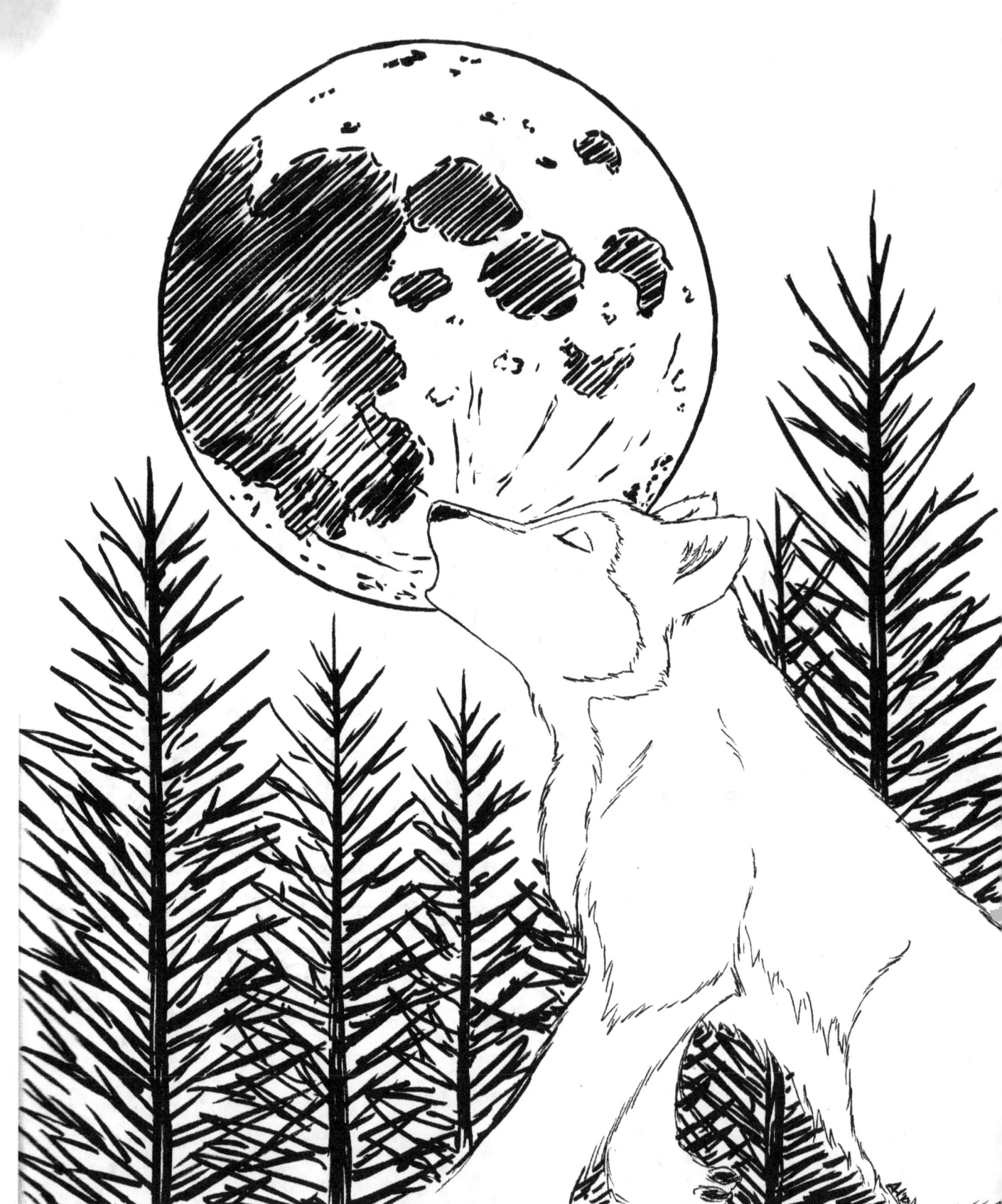

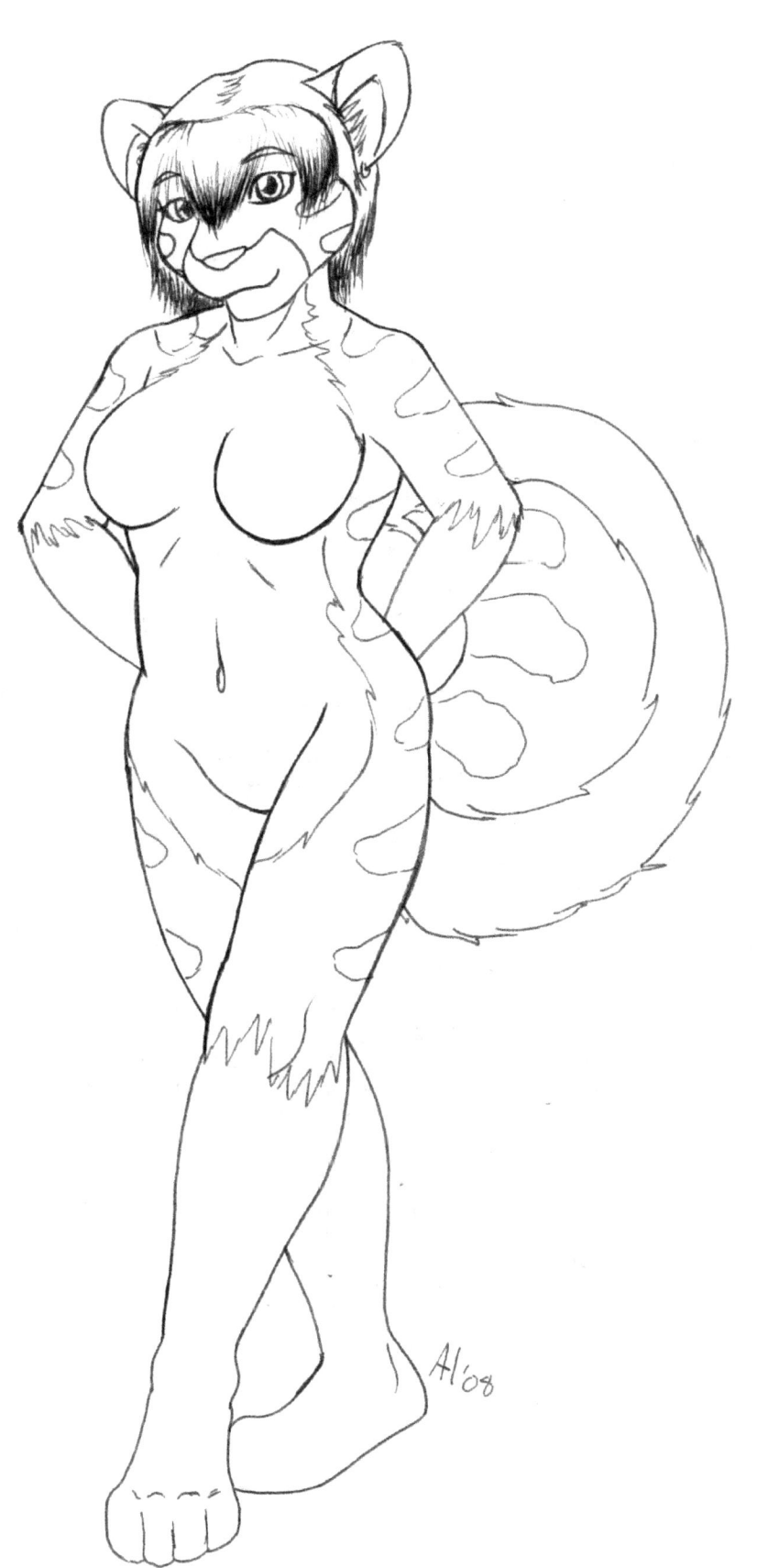

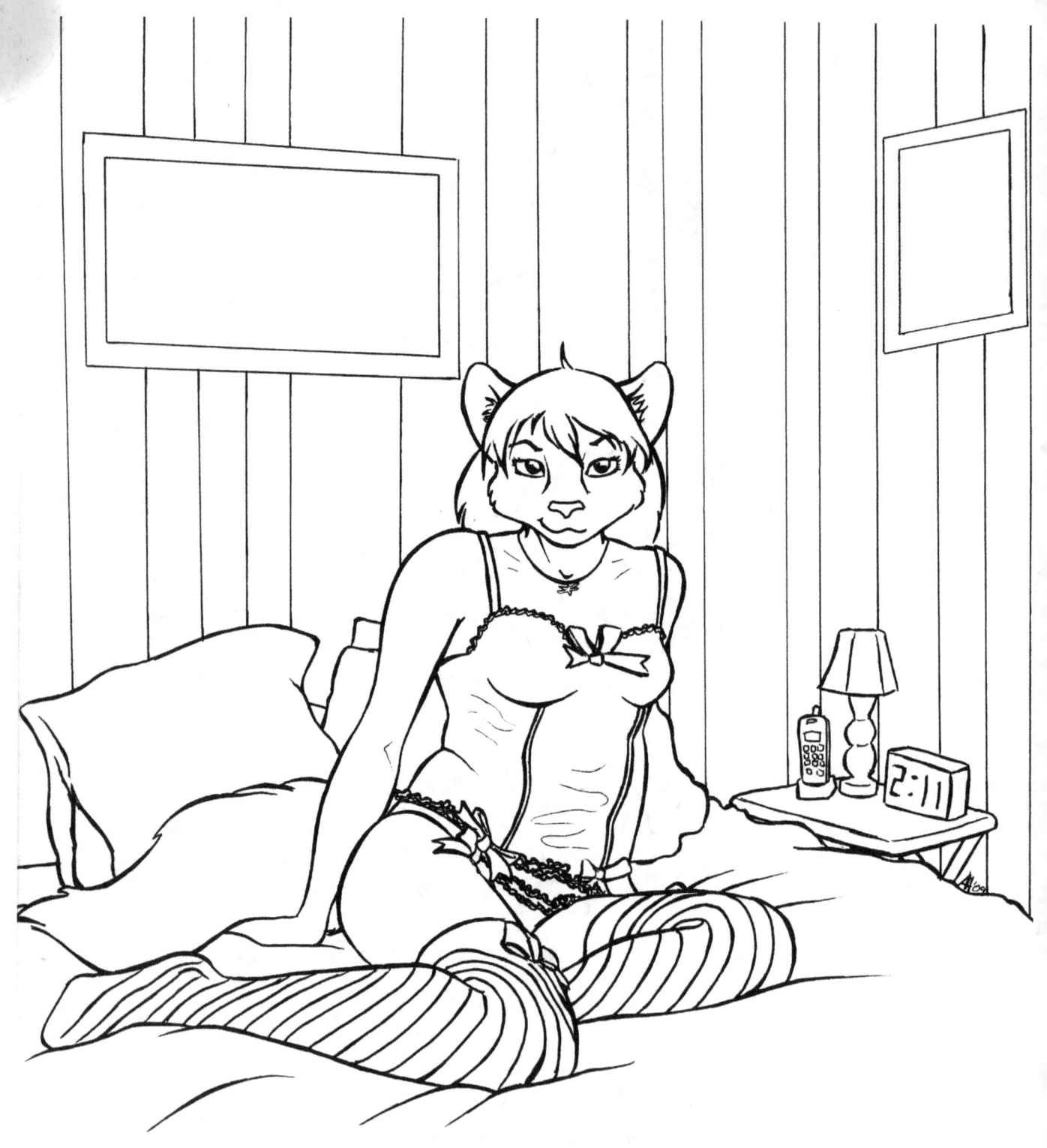

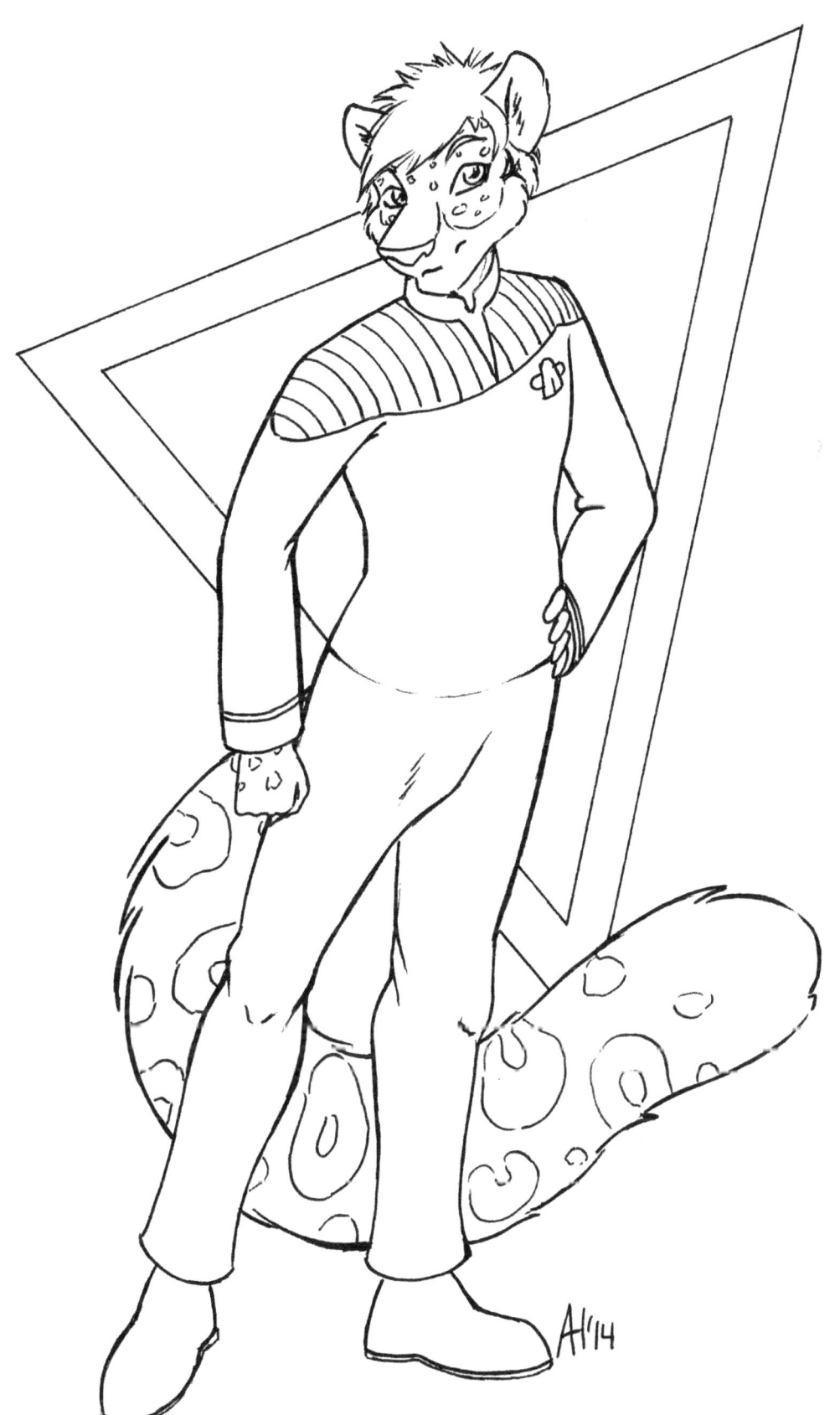

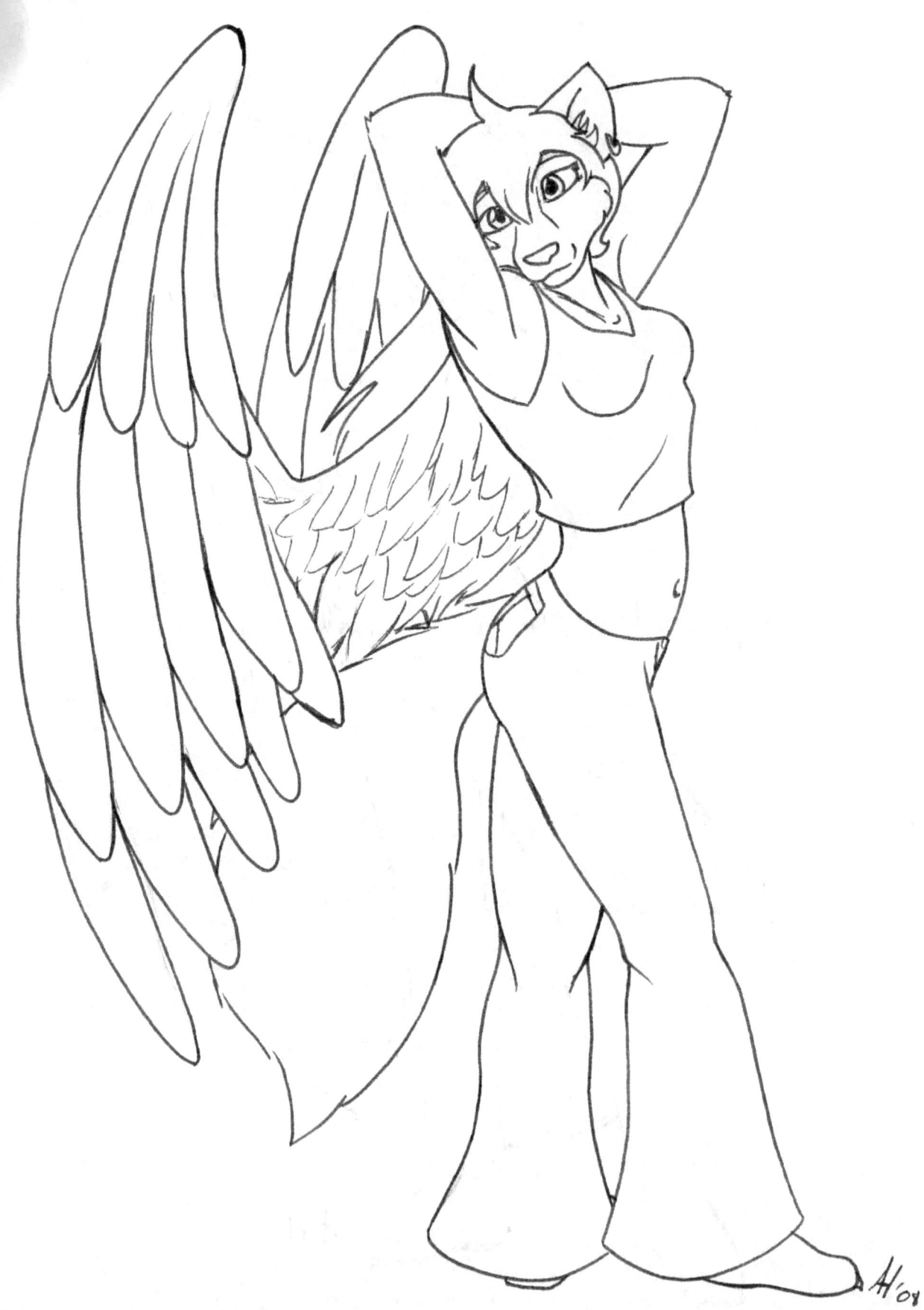

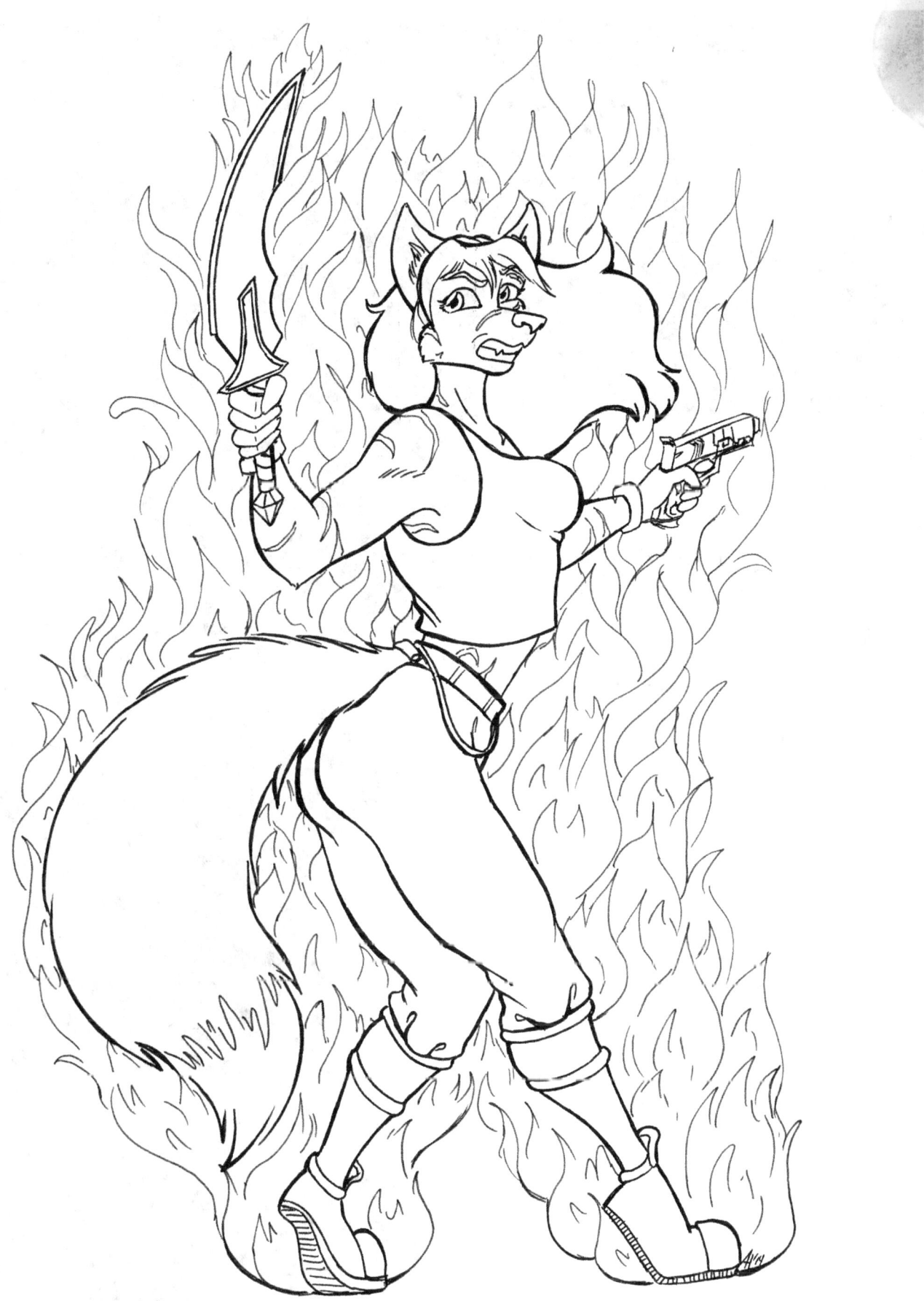

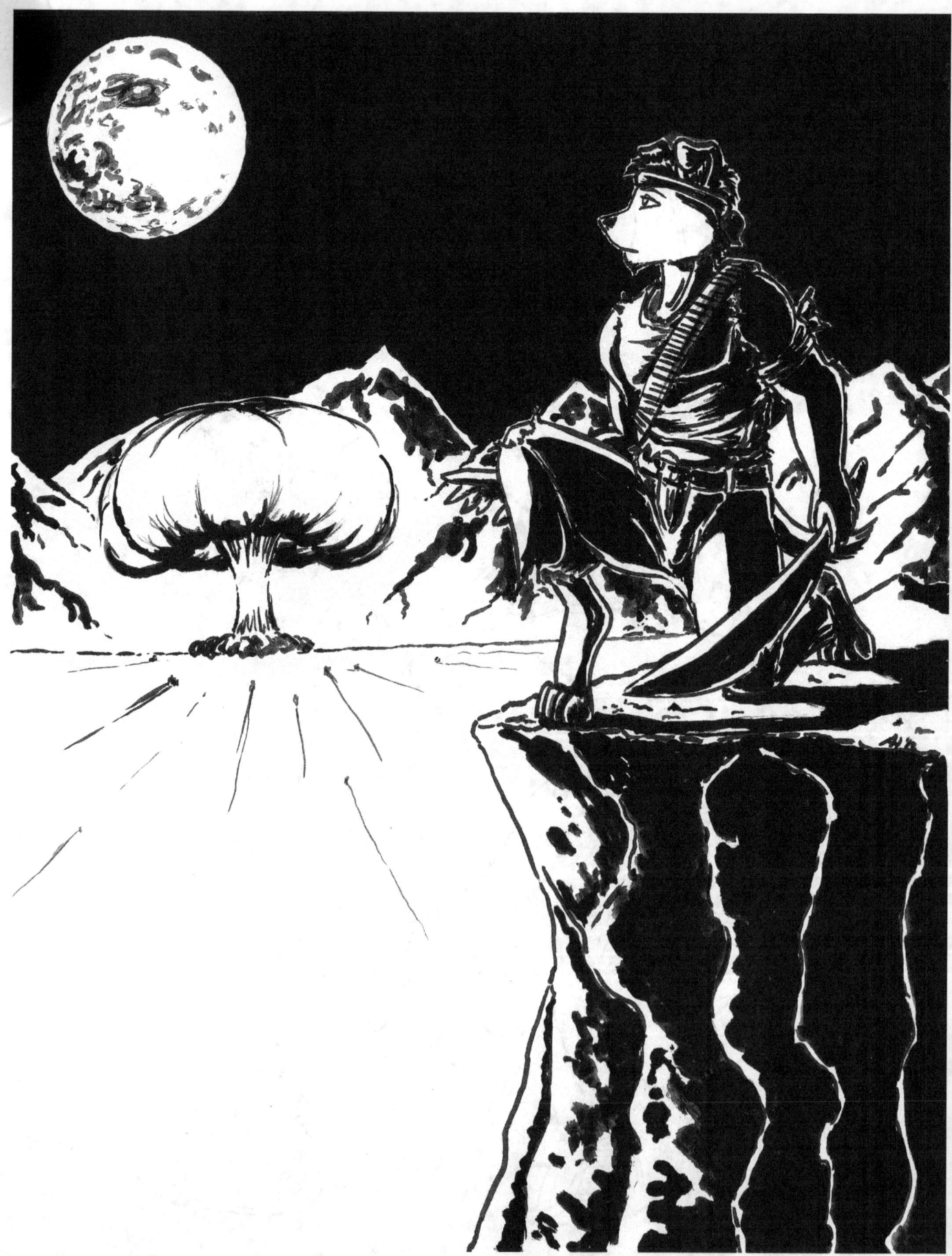

WANT TO SHARE YOUR MASTERPIECE? SEND YOUR COLORED DRAWINGS TO:

ASHLEY@ALOPEXSTUDIOS.COM

YOUR DRAWINGS MAY BE REPRODUCED PUBLICLY, AND YOU WILL BE CREDITED, UNLESS YOU DON'T WANT TO BE.

FIND MORE OF MY WORK AT:

HTTP://WWW.ALOPEXSTUDIOS.COM
OR
HTTP:WWW.FURAFFINITY.NET/USER/ZANNAH

OR ON TWITTER:

@ASHOLOHAN

REGULAR LIVE ART STREAMS ON TIGERDILE:

HTTPS://ZANNAH.TIGERDILE.COM